Writing
from the
Heart

Other Books by Lesléa Newman

Novels:
Good Enough to Eat
In Every Laugh a Tear
Fat Chance

Short Story Collections:
A Letter to Harvey Milk
Secrets
Every Woman's Dream

Poetry Collections:
Love Me Like You Mean It
Sweet Dark Places
Still Life with Buddy

Humor:
Out of the Closet and Nothing to Wear

Non-fiction:
SomeBODY to Love: A Guide to Loving the Body You Have

Anthologies:
Bubbe Meisehs by Shayneh Maidelehs: Poetry by Jewish Grandaughters
    About Our Grandmothers
Eating Our Hearts Out: Personal Accounts of Women's Relationship to Food
A Loving Testimony: Remembering Loved Ones Lost to AIDS
The Femme Mystique
My Lover is a Woman: Contemporary Lesbian Love Poems

Children's Books:
Heather Has Two Mommies
Gloria Goes to Gay Pride
Belinda's Bouquet
Saturday is Pattyday
Too Far Away to Touch
Remember That

Writing
from the
Heart

Inspiration and Exercises for
Women Who Want to Write

by
Lesléa Newman

❋

The Crossing Press, Freedom, CA 95019

For My Students
with thanks for all you've taught me

Copyright © 1993 by Lesléa Newman
Cover design by David Charlsen
Book design by Carolyn Saso
Printed in the U.S.A
5th Printing 1999

Library of Congress Cataloging-in-Publication Data

Newman, Lesléa.
    Writing from the heart : inspiration and exercises for women who
want to write / by Lesléa Newman.
        p. cm.
    Includes bibliographical references.
    ISBN 0-89594-641-6 (paper)
    1. Authorship. 2. Fiction--Women authors--Technique. I. Title.
PN151.N38 1993
808.3--dc20

                                      93-25551
                                         CIP

Contents

What would happen if one woman
told the truth about her life?
The world would split open.

Muriel Rukeyser

Introduction

Writing From The Heart is a book for women who want to write but think they have nothing to say, or women who know they have something to say but don't know how to say it. As women, many of us have been told that our words aren't important. We have been told time and again that what we have to say doesn't matter. We have been told that we are too young to write, too old to write, too dumb to write, too sentimental to write, too hysterical, too sad, too angry, too insignificant, too female to write. It takes work and courage to hush these voices that have taken up residence in our brains and declare, "You're wrong. I do have something to say." Often when a woman gets this far, she faces another hurdle: the voice that says, "All right, maybe you do have something to say. Go ahead and write if you want, but you know it's not going to be any good."

NOW HEAR THIS: every woman has important stories to tell and the ability to tell them. There are no exceptions. Not even you. I have been teaching women's writing workshops for the past ten years, and out of the hundreds of women I have been privileged to work with, I have never met one who had nothing to say. On the contrary, after taking a "Write from the Heart" workshop, many women who had started out saying, "I have nothing to write about" wound up declaring, "I have so much to write about, I don't know where to start!"

Writers are not special. Rather, every woman has the potential to be a special writer. This contradicts everything most of us have been taught. I learned early on that writers were indeed special; they were ultrasensitive, they had to be tiptoed around and handled with kid gloves. I also learned that writers were mostly male. If you happened to be female, your chances of being a successful writer increased if you were depressed, or preferably dead. When I was in a graduate writing program in 1981, there were two portraits hanging on the walls of the student writing lounge: one of Sylvia Plath and one of Anne Sexton. These two fine poets both committed suicide. While I can admire their work, they are not who I would pick as role models.

I am now my own role model. I know I don't have to be depressed or dead or an alcoholic in an ivory tower or a junkie on skid row or any other "romantic" image of a writer in order to write. My life is quite ordinary. I get up, shower, dress, eat breakfast and sit down to write at 9:15 five mornings a week. I write all morning, break for lunch, and continue writing for part of the afternoon. Around 3:30 p.m. I leave my study to do "writing errands," which usually involve a trip to the post office, stationery store and copy shop. I come home, share dinner with my spouse and teach writing classes four nights a week. Then I read or watch TV, perhaps have a snack and go to bed.

Sound pretty ordinary? Throw in doing the laundry, going grocery shopping, paying the bills and taking the cat to the vet, and I'll bet my life sounds pretty much like yours. In fact, you may be wondering right now, "What in the world does she have to write about?"

Nothing much. Absolutely everything. The stuff of my life which is ordinary, yet extraordinary. I have met many women who think they can't be writers because their lives aren't interesting enough to write about. This is simply untrue. Everyone's life is mysterious, beautiful, stunning magic. It doesn't matter if you've lived in the same town your whole life or traveled around the world seven times. What matters is your ability to open up to the breathtaking and spectacular adventure that happens to be your life. Your job is to experience it, see it, feel it, live it and write it down.

Think about what happens when you travel to a foreign country or even the next town over. Your eyes are open wide. You see new things, hear new sounds, taste new foods. Everything seems so alive, so exciting, so interesting. Yet to the people who live in that country or town, it is just another ordinary day.

In 1977, I was hitchhiking through Europe and found myself in a small town in Italy. One day as I stood on the sidewalk, I watched a woman lower a picnic basket down from her second-story window to a young man who placed a loaf of bread in it. The woman pulled her basket up by a rope and that was the end of it. To her, I'm sure it was no big deal, just something she did every day. But I found this method of obtaining bread wonderfully interesting (so much so that here I am fifteen years later writing about it!).

Your life is full of interesting moments like these. To be a writer, you must become a tourist and explore the country of your own life. See every day, every minute of your life as if it is brand new. For it is. Even if you are writing about something you have done 1,000 times before, like drinking a cup of coffee, try to experience it as if it's the first time. Because it is, you know. Even if you've drunk 1,000 cups of coffee, this is the first time you are drinking cup of coffee #1,001. How is it different from all the other cups of coffee that have preceded it? Is it in a different cup, are you sitting at a different table, are you talking to someone new? Even if you have sat at the same kitchen table drinking coffee out of the same mug all by yourself every day for the past ten years, somehow today's experience of drinking coffee will be unique and interesting. Is there a bird outside your window? A new song on the radio? A patch of sunlight falling across the table? A wild thought in your mind?

Every single day of your life is full of interesting material to write about. A wonderful example of this concept is Alexander Solzhenitsyn's book *One Day in the Life of Ivan Denisovich*. This 158-page book tells the story of one day in the life of a man who is in a Stalinist work camp. The book starts when he wakes up and ends when he goes to sleep. It is an ordinary day; in fact the author tells us it is a day not unlike the other 3,653 days Ivan Denisovich spends in prison. Yet after reading about everything that goes on in the main character's life, including his dreams, hopes, fears, fantasies, memories, actions and interactions, it all seems quite extraordinary.

Bernadette Mayer's book *Midwinter Day* accomplishes the same goal. This 119-page poem tells the story of a day in the author's life, December 22. Again, the book portrays an ordinary human being going about her life on an ordinary day. Yet, her story is fascinating.

And so is yours. Every day of your life is a remarkably interesting sequence of thoughts, feelings, memories, dreams, events and interactions, worthy of writing down.

*   *   *

But what if I don't know where to start? Where do I begin?
Begin right here, from the place of not knowing. This is actually the best place to start. Absolutely. Also the scariest. Also the most exciting. Writing involves taking risks. If you know what you're going to write, there's no point in writing it. A common myth many women hold about writing is that we have to know what we're going to write before we write it. There goes the mystery, the challenge, the suspense, the fun.

Writing is about diving into the unknown. Your writing, if you let it, will lead you to new places deep inside yourself. Every time you write is an opportunity to learn something new—about the process of writing, about your characters, about the world, about yourself. One reason I enjoy writing so much is that it constantly surprises me. I may start off with an idea of where I want a particular piece of writing to go, but 99 percent of the time, the writing leads me somewhere else. Thus I am always learning, growing and being challenged in new and exciting ways.

This doesn't mean that everything I write turns into a successful story. It means I am involved in a process. Most good writers have full wastepaper baskets (or, in this day and age, perhaps I should say most good writers frequently use the Delete key on their word processors). Writers must be willing to explore uncharted territory. We try one thing, and if that doesn't work, we try something else. There is no formula for a good piece of writing. It is not like arithmetic where $2 + 2 = 4$. Subject plus verb plus direct and indirect object does not necessarily equal a fantastic sentence.

Every piece of writing has its own unique formula, its own set of rules that you make up as you go along. On any given day, I may write ten pages and come up with one paragraph that I find interesting enough to develop further. This does not mean I wasted my entire morning. I had to write nine and a half pages to get to that one paragraph. That was my process for that particular piece of writing on that particular day. On another day, I may write twenty-five pages and wind up with nothing. And on still another day, I may sit down and write a fabulous fifteen page story that barely needs any revisions at all. I never know what's going to happen when I sit down to write. The one thing I do know is that nothing will happen if I don't pick up my pen.

Writing is like any other artistic discipline. It takes practice. It *is* practice. Years ago, I decided to study another artistic discipline, one I didn't have so many expectations of, in order to learn something about artistic process. I chose karate. One of the things I learned was that every time I entered the karate studio, my experience would be unique. The first technique I was taught was something called a low block. It is an extremely simple, basic move, yet it is something even a karate master with a black belt practices her whole life. I saw that one day I could execute a gorgeous, precise, exquisite low block, and the next day my low block could be way off the mark. My wrist might be crooked, my elbow too elevated, my stance askew. Each time I practiced a low block, I was starting over. Even if I had done the same technique thousands of times before, there was always something new to learn from it.

Writing is exactly the same. You are always a beginner and you always will be. The day after you finish your brilliantly crafted, perfectly plotted, funny and heartrending novel, you are back to square one: a blank page. Again, you are at the beginning. Your past accomplishments are just that—past. You must start over and see what you have to say right now.

The scarecrow in *The Wizard of Oz* fears a book of matches more than anything else in the world. The thing that scares me more than anything is a blank page. Facing a blank page every morning takes all the courage I have and then some. All my fears rise to the surface. I'm afraid I'll have nothing to say, or I'm afraid that what I have to say won't be good enough or smart enough or funny enough. Or I'm afraid that what I have to say has already been said a thousand times before. Even with three novels, forty-four short stories, and one hundred thirty poems under my belt, I still feel this way fairly often. I suspect other women writers do, too. We have been well trained to doubt our worth and our talents. My solution is not to wait for the fears to vanish, for that could take forever. Instead, I take a deep breath (or two or three) and start writing anyway.

It is human nature to fear the unknown, and the unknown is exactly what a blank page represents to me. By filling a blank page with words, I get to know myself and what I keep locked away in the recesses of my heart and mind. More often than not, I will start off writing about one thing and end up writing about something else, something I had no idea was swimming close to the surface of my consciousness. If I truly let go and allow the writing to lead me, rather than struggle to control it, something interesting is guaranteed to happen on the page. Most of the women who have worked with me have had the same experience through their writing: uncovering pleasant and unpleasant memories, revealing hidden dreams and desires, unearthing unresolved anger and rage. It is scary and exciting work. You may not be pleased with everything you discover. Writing, like life, is not for the faint of heart, but it is always interesting.

* * *

How to begin? I tell the women in my workshops to start at the top of the page and work their way to the bottom. Just start writing. Don't think. Don't worry about the end product. Just relax and enjoy the process. Try not to have any expectations. When I write the first draft of anything (including this very book you are reading), I move my pen across the page and I literally do not stop until the piece I am writing naturally comes to a close, or a predetermined amount of time has passed. All I am doing at this point is getting my material out to see what it is I have to say. I don't go back over it and try to improve it at this point. I don't worry about the dialogue being authentic, the characters being convincing, all the verb tenses being correct. The process of going back over your work and making it the best it can be is not writing. It is rewriting. You cannot write and rewrite simultaneously. Writing involves keeping a steady forward motion. Rewriting involves going back over what you have just written with a friendly but critical eye. You cannot go forward and backward at the same time.

Often a new writer will confuse these two processes. I have worked with women who write one sentence and then cannot move forward to sentence #2 because sentence #1 isn't perfect yet. Somewhere we have been taught that if we can't do something perfectly, it is better not to do it at all. I urge you to begin writing with the notion that everything you write will not be perfect. You may write stiff dialogue or confusing character descriptions. Fine. How else will you learn and improve? Just keep the pen moving and put down something, anything. Then you have something to work with. (This, incidentally, is the only cure for writer's block.)

As a matter of fact, if you are a perfectionist, try writing a terrible story. Make it truly horrendous, with shallow characters, awkward dialogue, trite images and no plot. For many women I have worked with, this has been a breakthrough assignment, for it gives us permission to mess up. To have a good time. To relax. To write for the sheer pleasure of writing. To break all the rules and forget about the end result. To have fun.

For writing should be fun. There is deep pleasure in exploring your own heart and mind, pushing your limits, challenging your skills and mastering a craft. It is fun and it is also hard work.

*   *   *

Luckily, as a writer, you come equipped with a few basic tools to help you do this work. And for those of you who just read the preceding sentence and immediately thought, "But I'm not a writer," let me point out that a writer is simply one who writes. Do not confuse the words *writer* and *author*; an author is someone who has published a book. A writer is someone who writes. Since you are reading this book, I am going to give you the benefit of the doubt and assume you will be doing the writing exercises I suggest, thus writing, thus being a writer. So many of my students inform me they're not really writers, including one woman who had written in her journal faithfully, every single day for the past thirty-five years. If she isn't really a writer, who is?

As I see it, writers have three tools at our disposal. The first tool is the alphabet: those twenty-six letters that make up the words that make up the sentences that make up the paragraphs that make up the pages that make up the chapters that make up the books. Wow. Only twenty-six letters to express everything we all think, feel, do, remember, experience, dream and imagine. I am constantly amazed by that fact. Know words. Write them, rhyme them, say them, play with them, feel them. Fall in love with words and they will fall in love with you.

The second tool you have to help you with your writing is your senses. You want to convey to your reader the way things look, sound, smell, feel and taste. (A word about your reader: writing is more than self-expression; it is communication. Most of us write in order to be read. Hence your reader, or one who reads.) As a writer you are presenting your reader with a flat, two-dimensional surface: words on a page. What you want to do is create a three-dimensional world full of sights, sounds, smells, textures and tastes.

You want to carry your reader off on a grand adventure. She is no longer curled up on the couch in a fuzzy bathrobe with a steaming cup of hot chocolate beside her and a book in her lap. She is now high up in the snowy Rocky Mountains with the freezing wind biting her cheeks and whipping her hair against her face. Or she is now down in a damp, dark basement of an old apartment building, brushing aside cobwebs and squinting through the darkness in search of the fuse box. You want to transport your reader to another world, the world in which your story takes place. You don't want your reader to hear the clock on her wall ticking or her next-door neighbors making love. You want your reader to hear the voices of your characters growing louder as their argument escalates. You want your reader to hear horses' hooves clattering against the cobblestone landscape of your story. You want your reader to hear a torrential downpour drumming against a nylon tent even if she is reading your story in the middle of a drought.

How do you accomplish this? By involving the senses. The more sensory images appear in your writing, the more alive your writing will be. Think back to the time before you could speak, when you were a small infant. How did you take in the world? Through your eyes, ears, nose, mouth and skin. The senses are our primary language; this is how we still experience the world. Only now as adults, we have a spoken and written language as well.

So be specific in the sensory images you write about. Not a flower, but a rose. Not a rose, but a red rose. Remember cup of coffee #1,001? Again, how is this red rose different from every other red rose in the universe? How is this ordinary object extraordinary? Instead of a red rose, how about a rose, red as the polish on the ends of my mother's fingertips. Or be even more specific: a rose, red as the polish on the ends of my mother's fingertips the night she told us what happened to Daddy.

The more specific you can be in presenting an image, the clearer the picture will be in your reader's mind. And the clearer the picture, the more emotional impact your writing will have. Our senses are very connected to our emotions. For example, whenever I smell kasha frying, it reminds me of my grandmother and the wonderful kasha knishes she used to make. The memory makes me initially happy and then terribly sad, for my grandmother died several years ago. What brings up the joyful and sorrowful emotions in me is the sensory stimulus of smelling a particular food whose memory lives inside my heart.

Another example: suppose you are driving along in your car and an old Beatles song comes on the radio. You haven't heard this song in fifteen years, but, all of a sudden, your mind goes reeling back to the last time you heard it: there you are in your high school gym in a ridiculous hairdo slow-dancing with Jimmy Evans and pretending it doesn't hurt every time he steps on your foot. And all of a sudden you feel angry because he was a jerk, dating your best friend on the side; or you feel sad because he was a great guy and he was killed by a drunk driver two days after graduation. Whatever you feel was brought about by a sensory image, a specific song.

Even if you hadn't thought about Jimmy Evans in fifteen years, he rose to the surface of your mind unexpectedly and spontaneously because you heard a particular song.

This is exactly what you want your reader to experience. You want to hit your reader over the head with a clear sensory image that will evoke an emotional response. You want, for example, to write such a clear, specific description of a first kiss that your reader will remember her first kiss and sympathize with your character, even if your reader is nothing like that character.

This is an important concept to understand. Many beginning writers think it is better to keep things vague so that everyone will be able to relate to their story. They think if they fill in too many details, their characters will be too specific, and only people similar to those characters will be able to relate to them. They're afraid their characters will not be universal. Actually, the exact opposite is true. If the writing is good enough (and by that I mean specific enough) I can empathize with a six-foot five skinny blond adolescent boy with sweaty palms out on his first date, even though I am a five-foot four round, brown-haired, far-from-adolescent woman who has been on many dates. If I can see what the character looks like, hear what his voice sounds like and feel the texture of his sweaty hands, he becomes human to me. And all humans have the same emotions. If you are specific enough in your writing and really capture the human qualities of a character, no matter what that character's sex, age, culture, race or experience, that character will become universal.

The third tool, and by far the most important, is your own heart and mind. Everything you've ever experienced, dreamed, felt, thought, imagined, remembered, done or fantasized makes you unique and will make your writing unique. This is the most precious gift you offer your reader: the gift of yourself.

In the writing workshops I teach, my students work on a specific writing exercise and then we go around the room and each reads what she wrote to the group. Often a woman will preface her piece by saying, "I'm not sure I want to read mine. It sounds different from everyone else's. I don't think I did it right."

Your writing should sound different from everyone else's for you are different from everyone else. In fact, I would seriously start to worry if all my students' writing sounded the same. One of the wonderful things about writing is that you cannot do it wrong. Whatever comes out of your pen or typewriter or word processor is exactly what you needed to write at that time. Even if you stick to the assignment at hand for only one sentence and then go off on a wild tangent, it doesn't matter. What matters is that you write what you need to write, for no one else in the entire world is able to do that. That is your job and your job alone.

*   *   *

Now that you know what your tools are, let's talk about habits. A good habit to get into is to set up a writing schedule for yourself and then stick to it. I suggest a half hour of writing for at least three days a week. I suggest a half hour because less than that won't give you enough time to get into anything, and more might seem overwhelming. And I suggest at least three days a week because writing is an artistic discipline that requires practice.

If this is not feasible for you, plan something that is. You know yourself and you know what you can manage. Err on the side of caution; you can always add more writing time if you'd like. The goal here is not to set up an impossible schedule ("I'll write for five hours a day, seven days a week") and then fail and then beat yourself up by saying, "See? I knew I could never be a writer." (Sound familiar? Women are so good at that!) The idea here is to come up with a plan you can succeed at so you feel good about yourself and your writing. Even if you can write for only half an hour once a week, that's fine. The important thing is to do it.

Commit yourself to a specific time to write. If you just say, "I'll write for a half an hour sometime this week," chances are it'll be Friday night before you know it and you won't have gotten around to your writing. All of a sudden the littlest things become more important than your writing: the button on your navy blue blouse that's been missing for three years needs to be sewn on today; or you have a pressing urge to transplant that begonia that outgrew its pot in 1973. This is why I suggest you pin yourself down. Make a commitment: "I will write from 9:00 to 9:30 this week on Monday, Wednesday and Friday." Otherwise it's too easy to procrastinate.

Make your writing a priority. Your writing is important. That's probably why it's hard to begin. Especially if writing is something you've wanted to do for a long time. It's scary to want to write for years and not do it (what if I never write?) but it's much scarier to start. You are opening a door and you don't know where it will lead you. I invite you to walk through that doorway and begin.

Another good habit to get into is to have a specific place to write. That place can be an entire study, a corner of your living room or a place at the kitchen table. Find a quiet place where you can be alone (when all else fails, there's always the bathroom). Some writers like to write in cafés or similar settings in the company of others, but my feeling is there are enough distractions in our own minds, so why add more?

Surround yourself with whatever nurtures your writing spirit. Honor the writer in you with time and space that is conducive to bringing her out. Hang pictures of your favorite writers up on the wall. Type out quotes from your favorite writers and hang them up, too. Buy a pen and notebook or a typewriter or a word processor you like. Take yourself seriously.

*   *   *

If you commit yourself to writing for a half hour (or more) on any given day, write for the entire time. Let the phone ring. The dog can wait for her walk. This time is for you.

Often when I write this is what happens: for the first ten minutes or so, I do what I call "kvetching on paper":

> I can't believe it. Another blank page. Why do I do this every morning? I should go out and get a real job. Maybe I should be a piano tuner. But I'm tone deaf. Oh well. I might as well write. But what do I have to write about?

After a while this gets boring and my writing moves on:

> Well, I guess I'll try to write about P. I can't believe he's dying of AIDS. He's only thirty years old. I can't imagine life without him. We lived together in Manhattan ten years ago.

Usually at this point I will have a tremendous urge for lunch, even though it's only 10:00 in the morning. Or I'll decide I've simply got to throw a wash into the machine. Or I'll remember a phone call that has to be made right now. After writing seriously for fifteen years, I now know that these feelings are signals, telling me I am uncomfortable sitting still. I'm scared to face what's happening on the page. But I do:

> Back in the days when AIDS was spelled with a "y" and came in a caramel cube that was chewy and supposed to help you lose weight, P. and I would walk the streets of New York for hours. Everywhere we went people would stare, for P. was the most beautiful person, male or female, in the entire world, with his olive skin, dark liquid eyes, and long, strong legs. Now when I wheel him up Seventh Avenue slowly, trying to avoid the bumps and cracks in the sidewalk so as not to jar his body and cause him any more pain, P. tries to shield his eyes from the sun with a pale hand too weak for him to lift, and once again everyone stares, but this time for a different reason . . .

Now I'm going somewhere. Somewhere that makes me scared, sad and anxious perhaps, but that's okay. Your writing is bound to make you uneasy at times, for it calls on all your emotions, especially if you're writing from the heart. You can do it. You are strong, brave and powerful, even if you feel weak, scared and small.

*   *   *

A few words about using this book. The directions for each writing exercise are followed by an example I have written to illustrate the instructions. There are also further writing suggestions and, in many cases, recommended readings. The exercises have been laid out in a specific order for a reason. You will get the most out of this book if you do the exercises in the order they appear.

Unless otherwise stated, spend twenty minutes on each exercise. In working with this book you will practice warm-up exercises to get you going and learn the components of writing fiction: place, action, character, monologue, dialogue, point of view and plot. More importantly, you will learn a great deal about yourself.

But will this book make me a writer? More than one woman has asked me if I can teach her to be a writer. As I have said, a writer is one who writes, and whether you write or not is up to you. As far as being a professional writer goes, I do believe there is such a thing called talent, and we are all blessed with our own gifts. I also believe in hard work. Writing is 10 percent inspiration, 85 percent perspiration and 5 percent magic. Most of us don't work hard at something unless we want to.

The desire to write is something that cannot be taught. I suspect you have the desire to write or else you never would have picked up this book. Combine that desire with hard work and an open heart and mind and you will be well on your way to becoming the writer that only you can be.

I will now leave you to the writing exercises, for they, along with a blank piece of paper, are your greatest teachers. You do have something to say and you are capable of saying it. Trust me. Or better yet, trust yourself.

We need your words. Only you can tell the true story of your own life. Every woman deserves to have her voice heard. So pick up your pen, take a deep breath and split the world open.

1

Warm-ups: Getting Started

The exercises in this section of *Writing From The Heart* are designed to help you get in the habit of writing, have fun and start to discover the treasure chest of stories buried inside you. Try to do these exercises without any expectations of the end result. Relax into your writing and let it lead you where it may.

Free Writing

Assignment

Free writing, also called sudden writing or spontaneous writing, is a technique in which you write for a certain amount of time without stopping. Free writing is not speed writing. The idea is not to write as fast as you can, but to write continuously. If you get stuck, don't stop and think about what to write next. Just continue writing. If you get really stuck, simply repeat the last word you wrote until you get unstuck and your writing moves forward again.

Example:

The cat is purring loudly on my lap. I have to hold up my notebook at an awkward angle as I write this, but I don't mind really. I hope someone will inconvenience herself for my sake when I'm one-hundred-and-forty years old—which is how old this cat would be if he were human. One-hundred-and-forty—who would want to live that long? My grandmother died when she was ninety-nine and a half, not wanting to make it to one hundred. If I live that long, I'll be obsolete; I'll be the only human being on the planet who still doesn't know how to use a computer. There I go again—terminal uniqueness. I remember the Terminal Café at the dock where you get the ferry to Staten Island. I always thought if I ever wrote a horror book, I'd include a creepy hangout called the Terminal Café. One cup of coffee and you never return. Isn't it amazing, the stuff that lives on in the unlimited hard disk of one's mind? Who needs a computer?

The cat has crawled off my lap and now lies next to me on the couch in a splash of sun. Sun, sun, sun, now what? I've only been writing for ten minutes. Ten down and ten to go. My clock is also shaped like a cat, decorated with rhinestones. The other day when I opened the front door, a beautiful all white cat with gold slow-blinking eyes was sitting there, right on the door mat. She was very silent and mysterious, and, as it was the fourth day of Chanukah, I thought she must be a magic cat, with a message. I'd never seen her before and I know all the cats in this neighborhood. She hung around me all day and then left and I haven't seen her since. Her presence made me completely happy and even though this sounds really trippy, I believe my grandmother somehow sent her to let me know that she's all right. I always miss my grandmother at Chanukah, and the tip-off was the cat's rhinestone collar. My grandmother, just like me, never leaves the house without something sparkly on.

Further suggestions: Free writing is a great warm-up, akin to a musician practicing her scales or an athlete stretching her muscles. Get in the habit of starting off your writing day with a glass of orange juice and twenty minutes of free writing. It's a good way to begin to understand the inner workings of your mind.

Directed Free Writing

Assignment

A slight variation of free writing is to start with a given word and see where that word takes you. Begin with the word, pomegranate.

Example: <u>Pomegranate</u>

Seeds. Red. Red juice staining my fingers like when you eat pistachio nuts. Even though we could get the ones that weren't dyed red we never did; they weren't real. Especially when me and Annie read somewhere that the reason pistachio nuts were dyed red was because they were the queen's favorite food and red was the royal color, so everything she ate had to be red. Can you imagine? Apples and cherries and strawberries. And pomegranates, of course. Jelly apples and cherry Life Savers. Meat barely cooked so it was still red and rare. Mashed potatoes cooked in red dye #2. Maraschino cherries. Cherry soda pop. Strawberry Quik. Tomato juice. There sure is a lot of red food. Raspberry jam. Cherry lollipops. Licorice. Red hots. Doesn't sound like the queen was very healthy. She probably drank red wine all the time. And had red roses on the table. Funny, I don't remember thinking about this when I was a kid. I remember sometimes I'd get a nut that was hard to open and my nail would break instead. Ouch. Sometimes I'd get a bitter one and spit the little chunk of nut out in my hand. I wonder if the queen's fingers ever turned red from eating pistachio nuts. That would never do. She probably had a lady-in-waiting who would open all the nuts for her and put them in a little silver bowl. If we were kids again, we'd play queen and that's exactly what I'd make Annie do.

Further suggestions: Open a dictionary or any book at random, and write down the first word that catches your eye. Use that word to begin a piece of free writing. Do this on a regular basis every third or fourth time you practice free writing. Here are some "starter words" to choose from as well:

can opener	necktie	octopus
handkerchief	tampon	lavender
supermarket	chainsaw	pantyhose
belly	earthworm	high chair
flashlight	ice cream	telephone
speculum	Vaseline	pocketbook
pistol	teeth	garter belt
tangerine		

Writing About Objects

Assignment

For this writing exercise, you need a prop. Find an ordinary household object and place it in front of you where you can see it. Write about it in the following ways:

- describe the object
- write a memory about the object
- write a fantasy about the object
- write a monologue from the object's point of view (in other words, the object is speaking)

Take five minutes for each piece of writing.

Example: The telephone

Description: It is black and shiny like my grandmother's pocketbook, like my Mary Janes of old, like the black plastic garbage bags I keep under the sink. It has a round plastic dial with holes in it, like a flattened–out bowling ball gone bananas. There are numbers and letters on it, and one word: operator. It is heavy. When I look at it up close, I see myself reflected in it. There is a piece to pick up that is flat, with two bulges, one at each end. This piece has holes in it and emits a continuous sound when I press it to my ear. The piece has a curly umbilical cord attaching it to the square part on the table. The object is dark and quiet, though once in a while it screams.

Memory: I remember the phone ringing early in the morning and picking it up and some guy saying he really wanted to f—k me. I remember slamming down the receiver so hard that it made the phone ring again, a shorter ring like an echo, and I remember how sweaty my palm felt against the black plastic. I remember the next time the phone rang I spun around on my heel, my thumb and forefinger extended, like I was going to shoot it. I remember saying "hello" in a brusque manner and my friend Patty saying, "Lesléa?" I remember telling her what happened, the phone on my lap, its weight comforting, like a small child or a kitten, the receiver cradled between my neck and shoulder. After that I kept a silver whistle next to the phone, ready to blast off the ears of the next jerk that bothered me. But I've never used it.

Fantasy: The phone rings. It's the lottery people telling me I've won, I've won! The phone rings. It's my agent, telling me my novel is #1 on the *New York Sunday Times* best–seller list. The phone rings. My mother is on the other end telling me she loves me more than life itself. The phone rings. It is my grandmother, no longer dead, on her way over with a bottle of homemade borsht. The phone rings. It is the president telling me there will never be another war. The phone rings. The World Health Organization tells me they have found a cure for breast cancer and AIDS. The phone rings. It is a woman from the shelter telling me there are no more battered women or children anywhere. The phone rings. It is God telling me that this is not a dream.

Monologue: I'm a phone, what can I possibly have to say? No one speaks to me, they speak through me. I'm a medium. But you know what? Lots of times when people talk to each other, they don't really listen. It's true. They hold the phone away from their ear, or put the receiver down and go get a drink of water. Or they even pretend they have another call coming in, just so they can get off the phone!

I like sitting on her lap. I like it when she curls my cord around her little finger. I like to nestle up under her hair, close to her ear. I hate it when she drops me or trips over my cord. I hate when she unplugs me; I feel so useless. I get scared when she takes me into the bathroom and has a long talk while she soaks in the tub. I wish she'd polish me more so I wouldn't be so grimy and full of fingerprints. I hate when I ring and ring and ring and nobody's home.

Further suggestions: Practice writing in this way about the following objects:

- something from your kitchen
- something from your bedroom
- something from your living room
- something from your garage
- something from your toolbox
- something from your jewelry box
- something from your refrigerator

Recommended reading: "TELEPHONE I—XII," by Patricia Donegan, from her book *Without Warning.*

Writing About Personal Objects

Assignment

Personal objects, our things, the "stuff" of our lives. Why do we keep certain things around us? What memories do they hold for us? What stories do they have to tell? Pick an object that you feel emotionally attached to in some way. Write about five different times in your life you interacted with this object. Take five minutes for each writing.

Example: <u>My grandmother 's black beaded purse</u>

One: I am sleeping over at Grandma's house. After supper we play dress-up. I put on her silver high heels and a rhinestone necklace and she lets me carry her black beaded pocketbook all around the apartment. "I need money," I say, and she opens the bag because the clasp is too hard for me, and drops two nickels inside.

Two: My grandmother has asked me to bring her some things from the apartment. I do not know what she needs at the nursing home. I open all her dresser drawers, feeling like an intruder. In the bottom drawer I find the black bag covered with beads and sequins, lined with silk. I don't know why, but I decide to take it to her.

Three: "What did you bring me this for? What, you think I'm going dancing at my age? Let me see what else you got there. That blouse is good, and those slacks and those shoes. You take the bag, darling. I got a whole drawer full of evening bags, take them, take them all. Sure, you're young yet, you should enjoy them, go out and have a good time."

Four: M. and I are at a guest house in Maine. We get all dressed up for dinner; me in a black mini-dress and heels, she in a white silk blouse and black pants. There is a piano bar at the restaurant. We sit at it and I put my grandmother's black beaded bag down next to a lit candle. The candle is reflected a hundred times over in every single sequin and bead. I watch the flickering reflections while the pianist plays, "As Time Goes By."

Five: Nina comes over while her mother does errands. I am not used to having a two year old in my house and within five minutes the place is a complete disaster: cookie crumbs everywhere, dominoes scattered throughout three rooms, little boots kicked off in the kitchen, a bottle rolled under the couch. Nina points to my grandmother's evening bag collection which now hangs on my wall. "Pretty," she says, pointing to the black beaded bag. "Mine?" "You can play with it," I say, knowing my grandmother would want me to. I take the bag down and Nina pulls the handle up over her shoulder to parade proudly around the room.

Further suggestions: Write about the following objects in the same way:

- an object you love
- an object you hate
- an object you stole
- an object you received as a gift
- an object you found
- an object that belongs to someone else
- an object you want but can't have

Recommended reading: "Safekeeping," by Becky Birtha, from her book *For Nights Like This One*, describes different times in a character's life when she wears a certain ring.

Dreams

Assignment

Dreams are a wonderful way to get to know yourself and what is brewing deep within your heart and mind. Dreams can provide us with images we might not choose consciously; the subconscious is full of gems to be developed into stories.

Write down the last dream you had. Don't write it as a dream though; write it as a story and use the present tense as if it is happening right now.

Example:

My mother is sitting at the kitchen table in a shirtwaist dress. She is young, in her thirties and pretty. She tells me we have to move to Argentina. "I don't want to leave Northampton," I say. "We have a woman mayor and everything." But my mother is firm. She is already packing plates, bowls, glasses and silverware into cardboard boxes, wrapping each piece in newspaper. I am crying, my head on the table buried in my folded arms, but it doesn't matter. We have to move.

All of a sudden I am in New York City, on the Lower East Side, in a shoe box. I am very small, like a mouse and my shoe box is fully furnished, like a dollhouse. I see enormous feet go by, first a man's brown wingtip shoe, then a woman's black high heel. I wonder if it's my mother, looking for me.

Further suggestions: Keep a notebook by your bed and record your dreams every day for a week or longer. Use any dream of particular interest for the basis of a story.

Recommended reading: "In Dreams Begin Responsibilities," by Delmore Schwartz, from the book *Jewish American Stories,* is an incredibly powerful short story written as a dream.

I Remember

Assignment

This is an exercise I have done hundreds of times. It is a wonderful way to dive deep into yourself and explore the treasure chest of countless memories stored inside you. The concept is very simple. Write down the two words, "I remember" and then write down whatever pops into your mind. When that memory draws to a close, write down the words, "I remember" again, and begin a new memory. Remember to be as specific as possible; use the senses to describes how things looked, sounded, smelled, felt and tasted.

Example:

I remember crying when my mother made me give back the white Easter bonnet and matching white pocketbook with a lily on it because we were Jewish.

I remember holding a hot freshly-baked pretzel in one hand and a cold chocolate milkshake in the other hand, and one of my aunts saying, "Look, she doesn't know what to eat first."

I remember playing on the cold kitchen floor near my mother's legs. I would make two stacks of Green Giant canned vegetables and then lay a blue box of spaghetti across for a bridge.

I remember my uncle giving me a bubble pipe. I breathed in instead of out and the soap came into my mouth, making my eyes water and my throat tickle.

I remember playing with my mother's make-up when she wasn't home and somehow smearing some red lipstick on her green bedspread. I remember soap wouldn't take the stain out but nail polish remover did. Only it took the green dye off the bedspread, too.

I remember lying upstairs in bed on warm summer nights with the windows open, listening to the crickets outside and the muffled TV down the hall, and my mother and her friends laughing downstairs.

I remember playing fox and geese after supper with all the kids in the neighborhood except Myra whose father always made her lie down after eating for a half an hour to digest. We liked to ring her doorbell just to hear her father say, "Myra can't come out now. She's digesting."

Further suggestions: Write a string of "I remember's" every day for a week. This exercise, just like Free Writing, is an excellent way to start off your writing day. A slight variation: instead of "I remember" try:

- I see . . .
- I hear . . .
- I smell . . .
- I touch . . .
- I taste . . .

Recommended reading: I Remember, by Joe Brainard, is an entire book written in this manner.

I Remember (Directed)

Assignment

Another way to use the exercise, "I remember" is to tack on a third word and see where that takes you. Try the word, "red."

Example:

I remember red pointed nails at the ends of my mother's fingertips.

I remember the red eye of the burglar alarm glowing in the dark like a tiny monster's eye.

I remember the red blinking light of the answering machine, and imagining it saying, "Hurry, hurry, hurry."

I remember red jelly apples at the cider mill, smooth as stained glass.

I remember red cough drops that tasted like candy.

I remember red M&M's tasting better than brown ones but not really.

I remember Dorothy's red slippers in *The Wizard of Oz* really looking red when we finally got a color TV.

I remember red lip prints on my cheek when my grandmother kissed me hello. I hated them and would rub my skin with my fist trying to get rid of them, but oh what I wouldn't give for them now.

Further suggestions: Write a string of "I remembers," adding on the following words:

- I remember screaming
- I remember crying
- I remember dreaming
- I remember throwing
- I remembering loving
- I remember purple (or any other color)
- I remember Amy (or any other name)
- I don't remember

I Remember (Extended)

Assignment

Take one of your "I remember's" and write it out, putting in as many sensory images as possible. It's as if your memory is a scene from a movie and the camera is panning across the screen s-l-o-w-l-y. Write in the present tense, as though this memory is happening right now. Writing in the present tense brings the experience closer to you and will help you relive it as you write it. That, in turn, makes the experience more immediate to your reader, too.

Example: "I remember red jelly apples at the cider mill, smooth as stained glass."

Annie and I are walking home from school when she has this great idea. "Let's go get some apples at the cider mill." I say, "Okay," and off we go. The apples are all lined up on silver trays, upside down with popsicle sticks stuck in them. We each give Cathy Clark a dollar and take an apple. Cathy Clark is in our class and she works at the cider mill after school.

The jelly apple is delicious. It's hard and soft at the same time. Annie and I eat, not saying much. When we round the corner to our street, I start to get nervous. My mother will kill me if she catches me eating a jelly apple. I'm supposed to be on a diet.

I throw my half-eaten jelly apple into a neighbor's trash can and wipe my mouth with the back of my hand. When I get home my mother says, "Mrs. Bernstein called. What were you eating on the way home from school?"

Further suggestions: Practice expanding any of your "I remember's" that interest you. Remember to load your writing with as many sensory details as possible.

I Remember (Exaggeration)

Assignment

Now we will practice rewriting, as opposed to writing. Consider the previous assignment as a first draft. Now we will work with the material and come up with a piece of fiction.

Take what you just wrote and rewrite it, putting in as many exaggerations, fibs and downright lies as possible, in order to support the emotional truth of the story. This is what writing fiction is about: bending, shaping and molding the "facts" of a story in order to bring out the emotional truth of a situation. For example: Suppose you are watching a scary movie. A character who is deathly afraid of heights comes face to face with a stairway she must climb. At first, to you the movie viewer, the staircase looks ordinary. Then the angle of the camera shifts and the staircase looks impossibly steep and frightening. Now we are seeing the staircase through the character's eyes. The film maker is distorting the fact of the staircase to present the character's emotional truth regarding the situation. This is what writers do, too.

Recently while in New York City, I took a cab and the driver asked me what I did.

"I'm a writer," I said.

"What do you write?" he asked.

"Fiction," I answered.

"Ah, lies!" he exclaimed.

I was immensely pleased. "Exactly."

Rewrite your expanded "I remember" and lie your head off. It's great fun and very freeing to shape and mold "the truth." Remember to write your story in the present tense.

Example:

Annie and I are walking home from school when she has this great idea. "Let's go get apples at the cider mill." I say, "Okay," and we run across the street, barely escaping being run over by a huge truck that looks like it's carrying nuclear waste or worse.

But it's worth it, because there are the jelly apples all lined up in perfectly straight rows on a silver tray, red and shiny as Dorothy's slippers in *The Wizard of Oz*. Each one has a popsicle stick stuck in it like a finger, beckoning, "Take me. Take me." I'm practically drooling and Annie gets mad because it takes me like twenty minutes to decide which is the best one.

Finally we each give Cathy Clark a dollar and take an apple. Cathy Clark is in our class and she once did an oral report on making jelly apples for Science. You have to get the temperature just right or the jelly won't harden. Then you dip the apples. Once the jelly splashed and burned Cathy's wrist. Now she has a scar like she tried to kill herself and she never wears short sleeves anymore, not even in summer.

The first bite of the jelly apple almost breaks my teeth. The jelly is hard as glass or ice. Underneath, the apple is soft and mushy, almost like it's gone bad, but it hasn't. I like licking the jelly part; it's like an ice cream cone that never ends. And when I do bite it, the crunching is so loud, it's like a car crash is going on inside my mouth.

When me and Annie round the corner to our block, I put on a baseball cap and a pair of sunglasses so my mother won't recognize me if she happens to be looking out the window. My mother will kill me, or worse, if she catches me eating this. I'm supposed to be on a diet and my mother monitors everything that enters my mouth. She packs me a low-calorie lunch every day that is really nauseating: two carrot sticks, two celery sticks, three Ritz crackers and one ounce of cheese. Sometimes, Annie shares her lunch with me. She always gets something great, like a homemade meatball sandwich and a brownie or two chocolate chip cookies for dessert.

When we're only three houses away from mine, I throw my half-eaten jelly apple in a neighbor's trash can and get to work. First I spit into a bandana and wipe my face and hands. Then I take some dental floss and run it through my teeth. Finally I remove my disguise. Annie says I look okay so I go home. The minute I walk into the house my mother shrieks, "Mrs. Bernstein saw you eating a jelly apple when she was out walking her dog. A jelly apple! That has at least five hundred calories. What is wrong with you?"

Further suggestions: Keep working with your "I remember's." Compile lists of them, expand them and exaggerate them in order to speak your truth.

Recommended reading: "Eleven," by Sandra Cisneros, from her book *Woman Hollering Creek,* is a wonderful short story about a childhood memory of something red.

Simile and Metaphor

Assignment

In the last example of writing, you may have noticed images expressed as comparisons: "jelly apples . . . red and shiny as Dorothy's slippers in *The Wizard of Oz*." These comparisons are called similes and metaphors. A simile is a comparison that uses the words "like" or "as"; a metaphor is a comparison that doesn't. For example, "Your eyes are like stars," is a simile; "Your eyes are two shining stars," is a metaphor.

Using similes and metaphors helps your writing come alive and gives your readers visual pictures. It also helps you, the writer, come up with new and exciting ways of describing things and keeps you in the practice of seeing things as if for the first time.

For this exercise, choose any ordinary object you have in your house and place it in front of you. Pretend you have never seen the object before and come up with as many images as you can to describe the object.

Example: A small, round brown potato

A dried-up planet

A dinosaur egg

A chunk of desert

An ancient baseball

A brown meteorite

A tiny monster, curled up in fetal position

A sunspot that escaped from the sun

A three-dimensional withered cheek

A lost moon

A lucky stone in God's pocket

An inside-out cave

An old sleeping creature, its back to me, with head and tail tucked

A petrified meatball

An old woman's kneecap

The earth, after mankind gets through with it

Further suggestions: Place the following objects in front of you and practice writing images they evoke:

- a fruit or vegetable
- a kitchen utensil
- a carpenter's tool
- a piece of jewelry
- a piece of clothing
- a toy
- a plant, a rock or shell

Recommended reading: "In the Root Cellar," by Maxine Kumin, from her book *House, Bridge, Fountain, Gate,* is a poem that describes a variety of vegetables using similes and metaphors.

Lists: Pleasure

Assignment

This is an important exercise, for many women I have worked with tell me they can only write when they're depressed. If that's the case, why would anyone want to write? It is important to write about all our experiences, the pleasures and the pain. If you only write when you're depressed, it is particularly important to keep a regular writing schedule so you'll force yourself to write even on the days you feel terrific!

Make a list of at least a dozen activities that give you pleasure. Choose one activity and describe it in such a detailed way that your reader will feel the same pleasure that you experience as this ordinary activity becomes extraordinary. An example of a list follows:

- taking a hot bath
- reading the mail
- reading the newspaper
- eating a delicious meal
- talking on the phone with a good friend
- reading a good book
- writing a good book
- shopping
- petting the cat
- getting dressed up to go out somewhere special
- going for a long drive to no place in particular
- getting or giving a massage

Example: Petting the Cat

I sit on the sofa and immediately the cat runs up to investigate. First she sniffs the tip of my boot, then she raises herself up on her two back legs to smell the knee of my jeans. Will I pass inspection? I dare not move. After a minute the cat leaps up gracefully into my lap. I open my arms, letting her decide how she wants to position herself. She walks around in a circle twice and then nuzzles into my elbow, kneading my sweater with her paws, keeping her claws retracted. I pet her between the ears and then down her back. She is warm and heavy on my lap, her weight comforting like a small child's. Her fur is soft and smooth to touch. She nuzzles into me deeper and I slink down on the couch, my body relaxing. I feel pleasantly sleepy all of a sudden, like I have just drunk a glass of warm milk. Nothing else in the world matters right now: not the bills that have to be paid, the pile of mail that needs to be sorted, the endless dilemma of what to have for supper. All that matters is this moment of silent calm, quiet except for the insistent purring of the cat that grows louder and louder until it seems as though it is coming out of my heart.

Further suggestions: Go down your list of pleasures and write each one out in great detail so your reader feels all the enjoyment you do when participating in this activity.

Recommended reading: "Six underrated pleasures," by Marge Piercy from her book *My Mother's Body*, vividly describes and celebrates the simple pleasures of folding sheets, picking pole beans, taking a hot bath, sleeping with cats, planting bulbs and canning.

Lists: Forbidden Activities

Assignment

In the previous writing exercise, you listed activities you have enjoyed. The activities are familiar to you; you have done them. Now, come up with a list of activities you have not done; activities that for various reasons are forbidden to you. The list may contain forbidden activities from your childhood and/or adult life. Again, come up with at least twelve. Then, pick one activity and describe yourself doing this activity. This time, instead of using your memory to help you write, you will be using your imagination.

- watching "The Three Stooges" on TV
- swearing
- telling my brother to drop dead
- eating cookies bought for my brother
- jumping on the bed
- telling a lie
- saying "shut up"
- having my own telephone
- dating anyone who wasn't Jewish
- cutting classes at school
- having friends over when my parents weren't home
- smoking cigarettes

Example: Smoking cigarettes

My parents aren't home. I'm bored. My brother is outside playing running bases with his friends. I don't know what to do with myself. I go downstairs to the kitchen, looking for . . . for I don't know what. I'm not really hungry and I know nobody's home.

My mother's cigarettes are lying on the counter. Chesterfield Kings. I pick up the pack and study it. I've never smoked a cigarette in my life. In fact, I'm always telling my mother how disgusting they are. The house always stinks of smoke, I say. One more nail in your coffin, I taunt whenever she lights up. That comment usually gets me sent to my room.

I can't figure out why my mother smokes. Maybe if I try it, I'll like it. They don't smell so bad when they're not lit. But what if I get addicted? What if I die of lung cancer? I decide to risk it.

I take out one cigarette and lay it flat in the palm of my hand. It has no filter so I guess it doesn't matter which end I light. There's a book of matches stuck in the cellophane of the pack. I stick the cigarette in my mouth, light a match to it and inhale. The match flares for a second and then goes out. I remove the cigarette from between my lips and investigate. The tip is glowing. I take a few puffs. What is the big deal here? I inhale harder and immediately begin to cough. My eyes water. I go into the bathroom, throw the stupid thing down the toilet and flush. Then I rinse my mouth with Listerine just in case and go back to the kitchen where I tuck the matches back into the cigarette pack, just as I found them.

I still don't get why my mother smokes. I guess it's one of those things that doesn't make any sense until you grow up. Like kissing.

Further suggestions: Go down your list of forbidden activities and describe each one in great detail. Even if the things on your list are activities you would never do, describe yourself doing them anyway. This is good practice in stretching your imagination.

Assignment

They say there's nothing like the first kiss. There's also nothing like the first time you get your period. Or sky dive. Or eat fried octopus. Or lie. When was the last time you did something for the first time? Describe what you did in great detail.

Example: <u>Going to the car wash</u>

I pull up to the car wash and roll down my window. After I hand the attendant six dollars, he grunts, "Neutral, no gas," in the same tone of voice the roller coaster man used to use as he strapped us in and said, "Hands in, no standing." My stomach lurches as the car is jerked forward through no effort of my own. The steering wheel moves slightly to the left by itself, as if my car is possessed.

A whirring noise sounds and then the car is being sprayed with water from all directions. Large strips of cloth, like giant blue lasagna noodles, descend and thwack against the car, which shudders. I inch forward, my mouth in a large round "O" like that kid in the movie, *Home Alone.*

Now huge spinning brushes buff the car, followed by more giant lasagna noodles. A blinking yellow sign to my left tries to warn me of something, but the water on my windshield blurs my vision. Now a huge vacuum cleaner-like thing descends and I fear it will crack my windshield but it stops an inch short and starts to suck up the water on the glass. My car is let off the tracks of the car wash and I imagine someone wringing his hands behind me and saying, "Good riddance," but I don't care because I am free.

I reach for the ignition to start the car, only to realize that it is on already. Whew! I shift into first and give the car some gas. The whole world looks brighter out of my windshield, like the first sunny day after a solid week of rain.

Further suggestions: Make a list of "firsts" common to most women, such as your first kiss, your first job, your first sexual experience. Also make a list of "firsts" that are particular to you. For example, if you are a carpenter, your list might include the first house you built. If you are an actress, your list could include the first time you walked out on a stage. Write a detailed description of every first on both your lists. Include as many sensory details as you can, so your reader feels all the wonder that you did the first time around.

Recommended reading: "Blood," by Cherie James in *Word of Mouth, Volume Two*, edited by Irene Zahava, tells of a girl getting her period for the first time.

Techniques of Writing Fiction

Now that you're all warmed up, we will move into practicing writing exercises that work toward the creation of a short story. I have broken fiction down into the components of place, action, character, monologue, dialogue, point of view and plot. As with the warm-ups, unless otherwise noted, spend twenty minutes on each exercise and write in free-writing style, never letting your pen stop.

2

Place: Where It's At

Every story happens somewhere. Having a strong sense of place in your writing is important because it grounds your characters and thus your reader in a specific environment. The three elements of place are: setting, local color and atmosphere.

Setting is simply location and time: New York City, 1993; Rosalyn's bedroom, 3:00 a.m.; the planet Axytl in the year 3000.

Local color has to do with consistency. Everything you place in your setting is chosen consciously and "matches" the location and time. For example, if your story takes place in a small women's college in New England in the fall, you would describe the campus full of old brick buildings nestled among the trees whose leaves were turning red, orange and gold. There would be students in jeans and sweaters milling about outside their dorm, the wind blowing their hair off their faces.

Now you wouldn't insert a horse and buggy driving by, nor would you describe a student in an old fashioned floor length dress complete with bustle. Nor would you describe a magnolia tree in full bloom, a student in a bikini sunbathing on the lawn, or anything else that wasn't consistent with this particular location and time.

The third component, atmosphere, is the emotional element of place. Atmosphere connects the setting and characters. Atmosphere describes how a place feels. An office on the fifty-eighth floor of a New York City skyscraper with computer printers clacking, telephones ringing off the hook and FAX machines going wild has a very different feeling than a cottage in the woods of Vermont with a cozy fire going and big fat snowflakes lazily drifting by the windows.

During the next week or so, try to be particularly aware of your surroundings at any given moment. Focus on what makes each place unique, interesting and exciting.

Assignment

The simplest way to practice writing about place is to describe wherever you are right now. Use your senses as much as possible to describe what you see, hear, smell, feel and taste.

Example:

The first thing I notice is the cat, curled into an upside down "C" with hind feet and head meeting, staring up at me with one green eye. He is lying on a white towel on a maroon couch. Above him hangs a spider plant with too many dangling offspring to count. In front of the couch is a brown wooden coffee table covered with books, papers, a Rolodex, a black telephone with its back to me, and a blue box of Kleenex, one tissue waving in the air like a sail full of wind.

I sit in an old brown easy chair and to my right stands a huge bookcase made of pine. There are hundreds of books on its shelves: slim volumes of poetry, fat novels, short story collections with covers every color of the rainbow. There is no smell in the room except for the cantaloupe odor of the mousse in my hair, and no sound except the slight whisper of the pen moving across the page. Wait—there is something else: the uneven yet steady tick of the KitKat clock on the wall. I can't see the clock because it is behind me, but its sound is so present it becomes absent, blending with all that is taken for granted, like the hum of a refrigerator that ceases to be noticed until it stops.

Further suggestions: Go to a variety of places and "sketch" in words what you see, hear, smell, feel and taste. Try places very familiar to you and places you have never been before, such as:

- a shopping mall
- Dunkin' Donuts at 1:00 a.m.
- a train or bus station
- the airport
- a public bathroom
- a friend's house

- your own bedroom
- the local library
- a bar
- a street corner
- a restaurant you eat in frequently
- the laundromat

Try also describing the same place several days in a row. See what you notice about it that you hadn't noticed before.

Recommended reading: The beginning passages of *Visions of Cody,* by Jack Kerouac, contain gorgeous "sketches" of an old diner, a B-movie house and an employment agency .

Where Have You Been?

Assignment

In this exercise, instead of using your observation skills, you will use your memory to help you describe place. Make a list of at least twelve places from your past you no longer have access to. Choose one and describe it with as many sensory details as possible.

- the apartment in Brooklyn I grew up in
- the ice cream shop I used to work in
- my old apartment on Hawley Street
- my college dorm room in Vermont
- the kibbutz in Israel I volunteered at
- my house in Colorado
- the day care center I worked at
- the Grand Canyon
- the hotel I stayed at in Puerto Rico
- a bookstore that went out of business
- my favorite coffee shop, also out of business

Example: The kibbutz

What I remember most about the kibbutz are the orange groves, which they called "Pardis," meaning "Paradise," and that pretty much describes it. The sky was blue, the air fresh, the leaves on the trees green. At 4:30 in the morning, the temperature was perfect; not yet hot, but warm enough to wear shorts and a T-shirt. A truck left me and other volunteers off at the orange groves six mornings a week.

I climbed up a wooden ladder with a canvas bag slung over my shoulder and started picking fruit. As I looked out over the tops of the trees, I thought, this is what the world must look like to God. All I could see were the tops of trees and the occasional blonde or brown heads of other volunteers.

Of course, the first orange of the day never went into my canvas bag. It went right into my mouth. The skins of the oranges were actually green, and tough under my insistent thumbnails. When I finally broke through the rind, the tangy, juicy smell instantly escaped and intoxicated me. The oranges were sweeter than any I had ever eaten back home. I tore the fruit from its rind with my teeth and let the juice drip down my chin.

When my bag was full, I'd climb down my ladder carefully and pour my bounty into a huge wooden crate already half full of green oranges. After about two hours, we'd take a break. By now, the sun was high in the sky and the other volunteers lay scattered on the ground between the rows of trees, covered with sweat and sticky with juice. I lay down on the grass, too, closed my eyes and listened to the conversations going on around me in Hebrew, French, Russian, Spanish and Danish. Occasionally a plane would drone by, drowning out all the words. After about twenty minutes, the head volunteer would blow his whistle, and I'd climb up on my ladder, on top of the world again.

Further suggestions: Write a detailed description of all the places on your list you can no longer visit except in your mind.

Recommended reading: *Paris, France* by Gertrude Stein is a delightful book in which the author interweaves childhood memories of Paris with anecdotes and observations of the city.

Assignment

Choose a place that is familiar to you and fully describe it by only using one of the five senses.

Example: <u>My Grandmother's Bedroom (described by sense of touch)</u>

I walk into her bedroom and pick up her downy pillow, burying my head into its feathers. It is soft as a cloud or a woman's body, but there is a heaviness to it, too. I sit on the bed which gives with my weight, being much softer than my bed at home and probably not used to the bulk of my body compared with my tiny grandmother. When I was a child, I would sleep next to her on my grandfather's side. Tonight, I will sleep here alone.

I open the top drawer of her dresser and take out one of her nightgowns. It slips over my shoulders and down my back, soft as a whisper that says, "Remember me." I look in the mirror over the dresser and touch my cloudy reflection. Dust tickles my fingertips; dust that would never be permitted by my grandmother if she were still alive.

I open another drawer, the drawer that holds all my grandmother's costume jewelry. I put on a rhinestone necklace, the jewels cool against my skin. I put on a bracelet of green stones, heavy against my wrist. Black earrings pinch my ear lobes and a poodle-shaped pin drags my nightgown. I want to touch everything: the small bottles of perfume that fit into the palm of my hand, the nylon stockings that run up my arm like silk, the cool cotton sheets in the bottom drawer, the black velvet yarmulke in her night table drawer that is soft as the night filling in the windows and settling heavily around my shoulders, reminding me once again that my grandmother is gone.

Further suggestions: Describe one place in the following ways:

- by sight only
- by sound only
- by smell only
- by touch only
- by taste only

Also try picking one of the five senses and practice describing different places by that one sense. (For example, using only the sense of smell, describe a public bathroom, a bakery, a paint store and a hospital).

Do this for all the senses.

Place: Implied Emotions

Assignment

Consider the following descriptions of the same place:

One: The walls were a putrid green and smelled like piss. The ceiling was old and cracked; I was afraid it would fall on my head any second.

Two: The walls were the same comforting green of my elementary school of long ago and there was a sticky, sweet smell in the air. The ceiling was old and cracked, like an ancient, much loved tea-cup held between two gentle hands.

Notice neither narrator says, "I love this place" or "I hate this place," yet her feelings are apparent. It is much more effective to *show* your reader how you feel through images and example rather than *tell* your readers how you feel through ideas and opinions.

Think of a place you have strong feelings about, and without telling your reader how you feel, describe the place in such a way that your feelings are obvious.

Example:

My apartment, and I use the term loosely, was one room, the size of a shoe box that belonged to someone with an extremely small foot. When Jay came over, he lay down right on the filthy rug that came with the place, stretched his hands and feet to the four corners of the room and said, "Now I've seen everything."

I ignored him and did my best though. Banging together a loft bed doubled my space and gave me a false sense of security that I was safe from the roaches that patrolled my pad nightly. Still, every night at the slightest rustle, I'd start up in bed, banging my head on the ceiling that was only a foot above my prone body.

Under the loft, I crammed a dresser for my clothes and a few milk crates that held my books and important papers. There wasn't room for much else except a radio that worked valiantly, though in vain, to drown out the noises from the street: fire engines and ambulances, trailer trucks, and, of course, other people's radios.

The room came with a tiny sink and a two–burner hot plate, though of course neither of the burners worked. No matter though.

This made the room officially an efficiency; thus more rent could be charged. Never mind that the bathroom was down a dark dingy hall that always smelled like cabbage and to get to it I had to pass Mr. B.'s room and listen to his hacking cough and spit. The bathroom was actually a closet with a toilet inside. When I sat down and closed the door, my knees banged the mirror someone had hung on the back of the door, and I am not a very tall person. Well, I would tell myself, sitting on that toilet and staring at my reflection in the cloudy mirror, this is New York. If you can make it here, you'll make it anywhere. But, I thought as I stood up, flushed and let myself back into my coffin of a room, if I can't make it here, does that mean I'll never make it anywhere at all?

Further suggestions: Write descriptions of the following places, never telling your reader how you feel, but showing your feelings through strong descriptions:

- a place you love
- a place you hate
- a place that thrills you
- a place that terrifies you
- a place that overwhelms you
- a place that embarrasses you
- a place you long for
- a place you feel claustrophobic in

Recommended reading: Cry, the Beloved Country, a novel by Alan Paton, opens with a gorgeous description of South Africa; the narrator's feelings about the land are quite obvious.

Place: As Relates to Character

Assignment

The environment of your story gives your characters something to respond to, and in that response something is revealed about that character. For example, let's say your story takes place in a supermarket. In walks a character who just had a miscarriage a week ago. How will she respond to this setting? The jars of baby food in aisle five may make her weep, and the woman at the checkout counter yelling at her son may enrage her.

In walks a second character in the throes of an eating disorder. She doesn't notice the baby food or the mother and child. She immediately goes over to the frozen food section and contemplates the calorie content of ice cream versus frozen yogurt versus sherbet versus Tofutti. Each character's response to the place they find themselves in reveals something about who they are.

Think of two people who have different feelings about the same place. Write a description of the place from each point of view. As in the previous exercise, don't tell how each one feels, but show their feelings through the description.

Example: <u>My grandmother's apartment, described by myself as a small child</u>

My grandmother's apartment is tiny. When you walk in, it feels like someone is putting their arms around you. There's always something that smells good going on in the kitchen: a pot of coffee boiling or a kugel baking in the oven. Grandma's kitchen is so small she can sit at the table and stir something on top of the stove at the same time!

Grandma's bedroom is down the hall. Her bed is soft as a marshmallow. She lets me wear one of her nightgowns when I sleep over. It's soft and smells like her.

We like to put our pajamas on and watch TV in the living room. Grandma has a big fancy red couch and when I sit on it I feel like a queen. We like to watch Lawrence Welk on TV. We turn it up loud so Grandma can hear. Once it was turned up so loud we didn't hear the phone ringing for ten minutes, but we didn't care. The phone is next to the television on this special chair that's kind of like my desk at school. It has a shelf attached to it for the phone and phone book. I wish we had one of those at our house. Our phone's high up on the wall where I can't reach it.

Example: The same apartment, described by a door-to-door salesman

I went into this old lady's apartment today—man was it tiny! I could barely turn around without bumping into something. The kitchen was so small, the old lady couldn't check what was in the oven without getting up from the table and pushing her chair all the way in. Whatever was cooking smelled burnt, so I was glad she didn't offer me any. The rest of the house smelled old, like water that flowers have been left in for too long.

We went into the living room and there was this faded old couch that used to be red, I guess. I was afraid to sit on it in case I would fall right through. The old lady's TV was ancient, with knobs on it and everything. No remote control in this house. And her telephone was a rotary dial, at least fifty years old. I can only imagine what the bedroom looked like. I tell you, I couldn't wait to get out of there and back to the twentieth century.

Further suggestions: Describe various places by different people who have strong feelings about these places.

- describe a house by all the people who live in it
- describe an office by all the people who work there
- describe a classroom by various students and the teacher
- also try describing a place in the voice of the same character at different points in her life. For example, how would a character describe the inside of a hospital on the day her first child was born, as opposed to the day her only brother dies?

Where Haven't You Been?

Assignment

In the previous exercises, you used your observation skills and your memory to describe various places. As a writer, you will at some point probably write a story set somewhere you haven't been. In this exercise you will be drawing on your imagination to describe a place you've never been. Remember to put in as many sensory details as possible, so this place comes alive.

Example: Undergarment factory, 1904

It is very, very noisy in here, with hundreds of sewing machines clacking away at once. Women of all ages, from as young as fourteen to as old as eighty, sit side by side, feeding yards of white fabric under the moving needles of their machines. The women sit so close to each other that sometimes their elbows bump. Every woman has a scarf tied around her head, and every woman's head is bent over her machine at a painful-looking angle. No one talks; even if they did, their words would never be heard anyway.

The walls of the factory are gray and dull looking. There are no windows and the air is stuffy. Bare light bulbs hang from cords overhead. Scraps of white fabric cover the old wooden floor as if there has been a snowstorm. As I walk down the aisle between two rows of machines, the tip of my boot lifts scattered remnants like fallen leaves, only they make no crunching sound.

I stop at my grandmother's sewing machine to watch her. One red curl has escaped from under her scarf and lies flat against her smooth forehead. She is the youngest one here, barely thirteen, and also one of the best workers. She doesn't even look up at me, her grown granddaughter visiting from the future, but keeps her head bent over the machine, concentrating on keeping her stitches smooth and even as the material streams between her small, strong hands.

Further suggestions: Practice writing descriptions of places you've never been, using your imagination to come up with clear, specific sensory details. Try describing:

- heaven
- hell

- the moon
- another planet
- your great-great grandmother's kitchen
- inside your favorite movie star's home
- any other time in history
- any country you haven't been to
- the inside of a space ship or submarine

Recommended reading: Any time a writer sets her story in the future, distant past, or anywhere besides the planet Earth, she must use her imagination to create a world where she has never been. Two examples that come to mind are *Patience and Sarah*, a novel by Isabel Miller set in New England in the nineteenth century, and "womanmansion" by Hattie Gossett, from her book *presenting . . . Sister No Blues*, which is the most wonderful description of heaven I have ever read.

3

Action: What's Happening?

Action involves motion. How do characters move through a story? What do they do, how do they do it and what do their actions reveal about them?

When writing about action, it is particularly important to pay attention to verbs. Verbs carry the action of a story. Be as precise as you can when choosing your verbs. For example, take the sentence:

Ellen walked into the room.

Now be more precise. Did Ellen strut, sashay, stroll, saunter, slither, sneak, slink, slide, glide, prance, bop, rush, run, leap, meander, mosey or waltz into the room? Let's say Ellen strutted into the room. But how?

Ellen strutted into the room confidently.

This tells you something, but not much. Adverbs are often shortcuts. You are *telling* the reader Ellen is confident, rather than *showing* it. What did you see in Ellen's movements that convinced you that she entered the room with confidence? Show what you observed rather than tell, and let your reader draw her own conclusion:

Ellen strutted into the room, her arms swinging at her sides, her steps loud and firm against the wooden floor, her head held high, and her dark green eyes meeting mine with a clear, direct gaze.

Now that's confident!

While we are focusing on action, be aware of how people, animals, and even objects move around you.

Directions

Assignment

This exercise will show you that even the simplest action is really a complex series of steps, which, when performed in a prescribed order, add up to that action. Make a list of twelve simple activities you know how to do really well. Choose one activity and write clear, step-by-step instructions so that anyone reading your instructions, would be able to perform this task.

- tying my shoes
- starting a car
- making microwave popcorn
- brushing my teeth
- making a phone call
- changing the kitty litter
- buying a book
- making the bed
- eating a sandwich
- sewing on a button
- ironing a blouse
- changing a light bulb

Example: How to make microwave popcorn:

1. Open box of Newman's Own Popcorn and take out one plastic bag.

2. Inside plastic bag you will find a brown paper bag. Snip plastic bag with scissors and remove paper bag. Do not open paper bag.

3. Look at front of microwave oven. Locate bar that says, "open." Press this bar. Door to microwave oven will open.

4. Put bag of popcorn on glass rotating dish located inside microwave oven. Make sure the side of the bag that says, "this side down" is facing down.

5. Close microwave oven door.

6. Press button on front of microwave door that says, "time."

7. Press the button that has the number 4 on it, and the button that has the number O on it twice. This tells the microwave oven to turn itself on for 4 minutes.

8. Press the button that says, "start."

9. Do not stand directly in front of microwave oven if you are nervous about radiation, but stay close to it in case you have to turn it off before the 4 minutes are up.

10. Watch the paper bag expand through the clear glass window on the door of the microwave oven.

11. Listen for the sound of popcorn kernels popping. This usually takes about a minute or so.

12. The kernels will pop one right after the other. Then the sounds of the popping will be further apart. When a kernel pops every 3 seconds or so, the popcorn is done. At this time, press the button on the front of the microwave oven that says, "stop."

13. Press the bar on the microwave oven that says, "open." When the door swings open, remove the bag of popcorn.

14. To open the bag, stand it up right. Take the two top corners of the bag and pull them apart at opposing angles from each other. To avoid getting burned by the hot steam that will rise from the popcorn once the bag is open, make sure you are not leaning directly over the bag,

15. Turn bag upside down over a large, empty bowl and fill the bowl with the popcorn.

16. Eat!

Further suggestions: Go down your list of activities and write step-by-step directions for each one. Make a list of more complicated activities you know how to do, such as changing the oil in your car or baking bread from scratch, and try those as well. Finally, try writing step-by-step instructions for a more abstract activity, such as How to Fall in Love, or How to Become a Wise Woman.

Recommended reading: Lorrie Moore's *Self-help* is a collection of short stories, many of which give directions. Of particular interest is "How to Become a Writer."

Work

Assignment

Make a list of all the jobs you've ever worked at. Choose one and write a description of what you actually did at that job, concentrating on your actions.

- delivering newspapers
- baby-sitting
- camp counselor
- model for life drawing classes
- selling crafts at street fairs
- short order cook
- ice cream scooper
- typist at a bank
- administrative assistant
- day care teacher
- journalist
- writing teacher

Example: Ice cream scooper

I turn to the window and ask through the screen, "Can I help you?" The man standing there asks for a double dip cone, chocolate and vanilla, with the chocolate on the bottom.

I turn and reach up to grab a cone from the dispenser hanging on the wall. Usually two or three crumble before I get a good one, but, this time, the first one I pull down remains intact.

I sidestep over to the freezer and remove a silver scoop that is soaking in a small metal trough of water. Next I bend over from the waist and start scraping away at the chocolate which is always rock hard, my elbow sticking straight up and moving back and forth like a broken wing. When my scoop is half full, I straighten up and deposit the ice cream into the bottom part of the cone. Then I bend over and start scratching away at the chocolate again.

When I have a decent amount of chocolate ice cream on the cone, I dip my scoop into the vanilla. It sinks straight down, as the vanilla is always soft as quicksand, and half my forearm disappears with it. I raise my arm which is now wet, sticky and freezing, and plop the vanilla ice cream on top of the chocolate. Then I hear the dreaded crack: the cone has crumbled. I drop my scoop into its trough and turn to pull another cone out of the dispenser. I turn cone #1 upside down and try to ease the ice cream onto cone #2 without crumbling the second cone or dropping the whole mess onto the floor. Somehow, I succeed.

I return to the window and slide the screen open to extend the ice cream cone to my customer, hoping he doesn't notice that the order of the ice cream is reversed. He fumbles with his money while a cold white drop of vanilla slides down my arm. Finally, he hands me a dollar and takes his cone without comment. One customer down, at least five hundred more to go before my day is done.

Further suggestions: Describe all the jobs on your list, including jobs you loved, jobs you hated, jobs that bored you, jobs that challenged you. Pay particular attention to your actions and movements.

Recommended reading: *If I Had A Hammer*, edited by Sandra Martz, is a collection of fiction and poetry about women's work. Also see *Working*, by Studs Terkel, a fascinating anthology of over one hundred people describing what they do at their jobs every day.

Observing a Scene

Assignment

Take your notebook and pen, or typewriter or word processor over to a window. Look out the window and write down what you see, focusing on what moves.

Example:

I see the brick building next door, a white car parked in front of it and the barren peach tree in our yard. Nothing is moving. Something must be moving. Yes, some clouds overhead are drifting through the blue sky and disappearing behind the brick building like a dream. There is potential movement: someone could come in or out of the building next door and start the white car. The dried up peach pits hanging from the tree could fall. The ice on the driveway could melt into puddles if the sun came out.

Still nothing moving but clouds. There's something: a woman walks by, one arm swinging, the other holding a leash. The brown dog she is walking trots beside her on very short legs, his upturned tail moving back and forth in a quick, steady rhythm, like a metronome. The woman turns her head and her long hair fans out behind her. They disappear from my sight. Again, stillness.

But not for long. I think I see someone looking out of the window of the house facing mine. It's hard to tell for sure because the window is full of a reflection of this house. Yes, now I can see, it's a man in a white shirt. He looks like a ghost. He folds his arms and looks out the window. Turns his head to the right. Unfolds his arms and puts his hands in the pockets of his jeans. Turns from the window and disappears into the room behind him. Stillness again, save for the clouds passing overhead.

Further suggestions: Practice looking out of a variety of windows and write down what you see. Try:

- every window of your house
- the window of a moving car
- a window on the top floor of a skyscraper
- a window overlooking a busy street

- a window overlooking a quiet country scene

Also try looking out the same window every day for a week and writing down what you see.

Recommended reading: In *Diary of a Pigeon Watcher,* by Doris Schwerin, the author observes the same pigeon family and their actions through her window over a long period of time.

Observing an Animal

Assignment

If you have a pet, observe your pet for twenty minutes and write down the animal's movements. If you don't have a pet, see if you can find an animal to observe, whether that be a friend's pet, a squirrel in a park, an animal at a zoo or pet store or a fly on the wall.

Example: Cat sitting on table in front of window

She is sitting. Her head is turned almost one hundred and eighty degrees so that she can lick her back. She bends her head further to lick the tip of her tail, her head bobbing up and down like those toy animals some people keep on the dashboards of their car. She interrupts herself to look out the window, untwisting herself, then spirals downward and licks the tip of her tail again. Then she stops and picks up her head to look out the window, first to the left, then to the right. Her left ear twitches. She looks up higher and then bends her head to her body to lick the front of her chest, her head bobbing once more. She stands up, turns around in a full circle and lies down, first lowering her hindquarters and sitting for the briefest of seconds, before letting the rest of her weight drop. She cranes her neck at something she sees out the window and makes a low gurgling noise in her throat. She tucks her front paws under her body and continues to stare out the window, motionless except for her body's slight expansion and contraction with every breath she takes. She is completely still for five minutes; I see she has fallen asleep.

Further suggestions: Observe different animals and describe their movements. Try observing a group of animals or the same animal several days in a row.

Recommended reading: The Fur Person, by May Sarton, contains many accurate and amusing descriptions of the comings and goings of a cat.

Assignment

Observe a person carrying out a simple task and write down what you see, focusing on action and motion.

Example: Melanie, cooking

Melanie squats down in front of the refrigerator, her knees angled out like a "V", one hand holding open the refrigerator door. "Any butter in the house?" she asks out loud. With the hand not holding the door, she pushes aside a plastic container of leftovers and half a cantaloupe wrapped in tin foil. A tub of margarine falls to the floor, rolls on its edge and then halts, upside down. Melanie lets go of the door, which swings shut, and picks up the tub of margarine. She turns it over, pries open the lid with her thumb and holds it under her nose for a sniff. She rises in one smooth motion and sidesteps over to the stove where a bowl of cooked rice and a frying pan are waiting. She lifts a spatula off a hook on the wall, wedges out a gob of margarine with it and plops the margarine into the frying pan. She turns on the flame with a quick flick of her wrist, rotating the knob that controls the fire ninety degrees. Then she tilts the pan by its handle, first to the right, then to the left, so the margarine melts and covers the pan evenly. The yellow square slides from side to side, becoming smaller and smaller until it disappears and the inside of the pan is covered with bubbling yellow fat. Now Melanie uses the spatula to scoop a large mound of rice out of the bowl. She drops it on top of the sizzling margarine and stirs the rice around, standing with all her weight on one foot, and her free hand in a fist at her hip. When the rice is done, she shuts the flame and lifts the frying pan to dump the rice back into the bowl it came out of. The rice slides out of the frying pan like snow melting off a roof. Melanie sticks the spatula into the rice, like a victorious flag, turns on her heel and walks away.

Further Suggestions: Observe different people doing a variety of activities and write down what you see, focusing on their movements. Try describing:

- someone you know very well
- a stranger
- a young child at play
- someone performing a task on TV (turn the sound off)
- someone at work
- someone playing a sport
- someone sleeping

Recommended reading: In "Preparing Dinner," by Evan Rubin, from *True To Life Adventure Stories, Volume II*, edited by Judy Grahn, the author painstakingly describes a character making a tuna fish sandwich.

Interaction

Assignment

We have been writing about people or animals doing things by themselves. Now we will practice writing about two characters interacting with each other. Go somewhere where you can observe two people interacting with each other, such as a restaurant or shopping mall. Watch them and write down what you see. Focus on what they are doing, rather than on what they are saying (there will be plenty of opportunities to practice writing dialogue later!).

Example: Two men in copy shop

The man behind the counter lays a piece of white paper flat on the black counter top. He is moving it this way and that way between his fingertips, trying to line it up precisely. He turns the paper sideways, cocks his head at an angle and squints his eyes to get a better look. He frowns, then bends from the waist, putting his face very close to the page. He adjusts the piece of paper slightly, and straightens up, nodding his head.

Another man breezes into the copy shop. He is holding a folder of paper in one hand and has his leather jacket flung over his shoulder, his finger looped inside the collar. He strides right up to the counter, says, "I have something to copy," and lifts his jacket which makes an arc over his shoulder and then comes crashing down on top of the piece of paper the other man has so carefully arranged.

The man behind the counter backs up. His mouth drops open. He stares at the leather jacket and then at the man who is looking down, shuffling through his papers. The man behind the counter turns beet red. He runs his hands through his brown greasy hair which ripples backwards and then flops forward. He shakes his head and starts tapping his right foot very fast, his hands on his hips. He flings his hands up and paces rapidly behind the counter while the other man takes a piece of paper out of his folder, looks at it, shakes his head, puts it back and lifts out another piece. He holds it out to the man behind the counter and asks for three copies. The man behind the counter snatches the paper, which makes a loud crackly noise like a pistol shot.

Further suggestions: Observe the following types of interactions and describe them, focusing on the action and motion you see.

- two people eating together
- an adult and a child interacting in some way
- two children interacting in some way
- a person and her pet
- two people fighting
- two people working together
- two people playing together
- one person helping another person in some way
- a group of three or more people interacting in some way

Recommended Rreading: "The Healer," by Sandy Boucher from the anthology *Hear the Silence,* edited by Irene Zahava, gives a detailed account of a woman giving another woman a massage.

Words of Action

Assignment

This exercise doesn't involve observing a person, animal or scene. Refer back to the beginning of this section, where I wrote the sentence, "Ellen walked into the room," and then rewrote it to make it more interesting and to reveal something about the character. Rewrite the following sentences in the same way, using strong verbs and specific images to make your writing come alive. Expand each sentence into a full paragraph, adding any details you deem necessary.

- She drank a cup of tea.
- She swept the floor.
- He washed out a cup.
- She left the house.
- He opened the window.
- She picked up the child.
- She threw the ball.
- She ate a roll.
- He called a friend.

Example: She drank a cup of tea

She cupped her hands around the warm mug and bent her head over it, letting the cinnamon-smelling steam rise and massage her forehead for a minute. Then she lifted her head and raised the mug in both hands, holding it with her elbows resting on the table. Her head moved forward until her mouth rested against the rim of the ceramic cup. Slowly she tilted the cup toward her and parted her lips, letting the warm, sweet liquid seep down her waiting throat.

Further suggestions: Look through a newspaper and find some short sentences that report action. ("Police removed stolen property at 8:00 a.m." "Mr. McArthur's car went off the road and struck a tree.") Practice rewriting these sentences with embellishment, to make the sentences more interesting and the action alive (this is just the opposite of what a reporter does; a reporter simply sticks to the facts). See if you can expand one sentence into an entire page.

4

Character: Who's Who

Who do you want to write about? Of all the elements of fiction, character is the most important. When I think about my life and what is most important to me, the first thing that comes to mind are the people I know and love. It's the same with writing fiction. The characters who people your story are what will concern you, move you, amuse you, intrigue you, inspire you and surprise you.

A character you choose to write about can be based on any of the following: yourself at any age, anyone you know, anyone you don't know (such as a famous person), a conglomeration of several people rolled into one, a perfect stranger, or someone you haven't a clue about and are making up as you go along.

The only essential ingredient in choosing a character to write about is that she be someone you love. (Note: I will be using the universal pronoun "she" to avoid the awkward "he/she" and the grammatically incorrect "they" when referring to a single character. However, feel free of course to write about characters of either gender.) Though you must love your characters, you don't necessarily have to like them. In fact, you may even hate some of your characters, but you must love them as well. One way to define love is "paying attention to." Thus, the opposite of love is not hate (which takes a lot of attention) but not caring at all. So when I say you must love your characters, what I mean is you must pay attention to them and care about them enough to notice every detail about them. Choose your characters carefully, as you will be spending a great deal of time with them.

If you are basing a character on yourself, I strongly suggest you change your character's name and other details about her (color of hair, height, color of eyes, number of siblings, occupation). This will allow you the freedom to let your character do anything she wants to and take on a life of her own, a life that in some ways will be similar and in some ways quite different from your own.

Your character is based on you, but she isn't you. Understanding this concept is crucial to writing fiction. Remember the concept of emotional truth versus factual truth which was discussed in the introduction to this book? More often than not, when writing a story based on something that happened to you, the story will be stronger if your character (who is based on you but isn't you) does something you did not do: what you were too scared to do or too angry to do or too shy to do; what you didn't have the guts to do; what you really wanted to do but couldn't; or what you never even thought of doing until you started writing the story down.

Likewise, if you are basing a character on someone you know other than yourself, it is important to change the character's name and other "facts" about her. For most of the following exercises, I will be writing examples involving a character who is based on my grandmother. (You may use the exercises in this section to develop one character in depth, or you may write about many characters.) My character's name is Zelda; she is eighty years old and her husband, whom she married when she was eighteen, died one year ago.

Zelda is not my grandmother; she is a fictional character, a figment of my imagination based on my grandmother. My own grandmother's name was Ruth; she didn't get married until she was twenty-seven, and her husband died in the thirty-eighth year of their marriage. But, more importantly, Zelda comes out of my own creativity and imagination. When, for example, I write about Zelda being alone in her apartment, I make up her thoughts, feelings and actions. Obviously, I have never been in my grandmother's apartment when she is alone (otherwise she wouldn't be alone). I have no idea what she felt, thought and did when she was by herself. And even when I was with her, I couldn't read her mind. So what I do when writing about Zelda is infuse her with my emotions: how I imagine I would feel at age eighty, alone in the apartment I shared with my spouse for sixty-two years.

I do not live inside my grandmother's heart and mind. Thus I create Zelda from my own experience and imagination. In changing her identity, I allow her to be quite different from the character she is based on. She may be stronger or weaker, angrier or sadder, more selfish or less independent. I really don't know what she'll be like until I start writing about her.

If you are writing about someone you don't know and are just making up—ah! What a wonderful place to begin. Your character is an open book (no pun intended) and you are bound to have less expectations and preconceived notions than if you were basing her on an actual person. Your character will reveal herself to you as you go along. Trust your character and trust your intuition. Go where your character leads you, even if you have no idea why your writing is heading in that direction. Your character will reveal herself to you in her own time.

Body Talk

Assignment

Your characters have bodies. They are not merely printed words on a flat page. It is important to know what your characters look like and how they live in their bodies day to day. Choose a character and describe one part of her body in great detail so that something about the character is revealed.

Example: _Zelda's hands_

Zelda's hands are folded in her lap. Her fingers are crooked and bony, gnarled like the branches of an ancient tree, and dotted with brown spots here and there. Her nails are painted bright red, like ten cherry jawbreakers. Every once in a while, she lifts her hands and they flutter in the air, as if they are searching for something, a pot to wash or a needle to thread.

Finding nothing, Zelda's hands settle back on her black polyester lap. Soon they begin patting the material, for these hands are not used to being idle. More often than not, there is a plate in one hand and a sponge in the other. A pail in one hand, the other holding a mop. Or her hands are full of groceries she carried up six flights of steps. Or her hands are busy shaping yards of cloth into a beautiful skirt for her granddaughter.

But today Zelda is at the doctor's. She sits in the waiting room and there is nothing to do but wait. Her hands reach for a magazine and pull it onto her lap. She licks the middle finger of her right hand and turns the glossy pages pretending to read; Zelda can't make out the words without her glasses which she's left at home. When she gets to the end of the magazine, Zelda closes it and lays her hands on top of it, right over left, her fingers turning her wedding ring round and round, reminding her there is no end to this, no way out of her new life as a widow, her new life alone.

Further suggestions: Choose a character and write about different parts of her body in such a way that something about the character is revealed. Try describing your character's:

- hands
- elbows
- ears
- feet

- neck
- back
- shoulders
- breasts

- knees
- nose
- mouth
- eyes

Also try describing several different characters by the same part of their body. (For example, describe Jane's shoulders, John's shoulders, Jean's shoulders.)

Recommended reading: In my own story, "A Letter To Harvey Milk," from a book of the same title, the seventy-seven year old narrator writes a description of his wife's hands in his journal.

If She Were . . .

Assignment

This exercise came out of a party game in which one person leaves the room and everyone else picks one person from the remaining group. The person who left returns and tries to guess who was picked by asking questions such as, "If this person was an animal, what kind of animal would she be?"

Choose a character and describe in detail what kind of animal your character would be.

Example:

Zelda is a mama lion. She lounges in the sun while her cubs play nearby, but at the first sign of danger she is up and alert, fiercely protective of her young. When the danger is past, Zelda licks her cubs' fur until they shine like gold. Then she tucks them in safely while she goes to hunt for food. She feeds her cubs all the choice bits and eats only what remains after they are satisfied.

Zelda is also a peacock with the finest feathers in the world. She likes to strut around and be admired. Zelda is a slumbering bear in the late afternoon, hibernating in front of the television. She is the early bird who catches the worm, the crow who is not too proud to scavenge and knows how to make a tasty meal from a rotten potato. She is a pigeon nesting in the eaves of an apartment building, impossible to get rid of. Her cooing gets on your nerves until one day the sound abruptly ends and you miss it terribly, wondering what could have happened to her and hoping she will soon return.

Further suggestions: Choose one character and describe her as if she was:

- an animal
- a planet
- a car
- a piece of furniture
- a room
- a country
- something to eat

- something to wear
- a song

Recommended reading: "i guess if i was a sound or if i was your woman," a wonderful poem by Sapphire, printed in the magazine *IKON*, second series #3.

Lists

Assignment

Making lists is a great way to get to know your character. Lists are not planned; they are generated as you go along. Choose one character and write the following lists for her:

- shopping list
- list of things to do
- list of her greatest fears

(spend five minutes on each list)

Example: Zelda's shopping list

From the butcher:

chicken, cut up nice

a little chopped meat to make hamburgers

From the bakery:

two bagels, soft ones

a few cookies, something chocolate

From the supermarket:

cottage cheese

bananas

carrots and celery for chicken soup

From the drugstore:

cold cream

denture cream

Alka Seltzer

From the store on the corner:

milk

orange juice

From Woolworth's:

white thread

knee hi nylons (package of three pairs)

Things to Do:

>   wash kitchen floor
>   knock on Sophie's door; make sure she's still alive
>   call my daughter; let her know I'm still alive
>   take heart pills
>   make chicken soup
>   go down on the Avenue and get some air
>   rest
>   watch Mike Douglas at 4:00
>   eat supper
>   wash out bloomers
>   try to sleep

Greatest fears:

>   falling on the Avenue and breaking a hip
>   falling in the bathtub and breaking a hip
>   becoming a burden
>   losing my mind and winding up in a nursing home, wearing diapers and babbling away in Yiddish
>   dying in my sleep
>   living in this world forever
>   not recognizing Murray when I finally meet him again in the world to come

Further suggestions: Choose a character and write the following lists for her. Spend five minutes on each list.

- List of secret desires
- List of reasons to live
- List of things she does in the dark
- List of most prized possessions
- List of people she loves
- List of people she hates
- List of presents she received on her last birthday
- List of things she likes about herself
- List of things she dislikes about herself

- List of what she is proud of
- List of what she is ashamed of

Recommended reading: "Things To Do" by Binnie Kirshenbaum from her book *Married Life and Other True Adventures,* is a short story in which the main character constantly makes lists in order to figure out her life.

------------------------------ *Objects* ------------------------------

Assignment

(For related writing exercises, see page 20 and page 23). The objects in your character's life tell something about her. Choose a character and describe something that belongs to her in such a way that something about the character is revealed. You may choose an ordinary household object, or an object that has special meaning for your character.

Example: <u>Zelda's refrigerator</u>

Zelda's refrigerator is a graying white hulk of a thing with a big, metal handle that goes ga-thunk when you pull it down to open it. There is a photograph of Zelda's favorite granddaughter taped to the refrigerator door. It is a black and white snapshot of a three year old girl sitting on a tricycle with a wide toothless grin. Deena is now twenty-two.

Inside, the refrigerator is crowded and smaller than you would expect. There is a white enamel pot of chicken soup covered with a plate; a pint of strawberries some of which are fuzzy; a carton of milk, a pitcher of orange juice, eggs, butter, cottage cheese, English muffins, apples and a plastic container of homemade egg salad, chopped very fine.

Down in the vegetable bin, there is a box of knishes from the bakery down the street which Zelda bought for her granddaughter Deena, who forgot to take them home. All right, she wouldn't take the soup, she was afraid it would spill in the car, that's all right, Zelda thinks, I can eat chicken until it's coming out of my ears, but what am I supposed to do with a dozen knishes?

So many years the ice box was empty, Zelda thinks, with not enough food to keep a bird alive, let alone a family of four. And now there's plenty of food and no one to feed. Murray was gone a whole year already, how could that be possible? The children were grown and the grandchildren had more important things to do than come all the way out to the end of Brooklyn to visit their grandmother.

Zelda shook her head and stared at the food. It was always the same with her granddaughter. Deena called and said she was coming, so Zelda bought enough food to feed the entire Israeli army and then Deena came and left after only two days, leaving Zelda with a full refrigerator and an empty heart.

Further suggestions: Choose a character and write about various objects that belong to that character. Describe the objects in such a way that something about the character is revealed. Try your character's:

- refrigerator
- medicine cabinet
- closet
- bed
- underwear drawer
- kitchen table
- favorite chair
- pair of shoes
- watch
- pocketbook or wallet
- lucky charm

Recommended reading: Ruthann Robson's, "When The Sky Is Not Sky Blue," from her book *Cecile,* is a short story in which a refrigerator plays a crucial role. "Janus," by Ann Beattie, from her book *Where You'll Find Me,* is a story about the relationship between a woman and a bowl.

Firsts

Assignment

(For related writing exercise, see page 39.) As previously stated, the first time you do anything is unlike any other time. Choose a character and describe a "first time" in her life that is a common experience (first day at school, first job, first kiss). Though the experience is common, each character experiences it in a unique way.

Example: <u>Zelda's first day at school</u>

Zelda's mother deposits her at the front door of the big brick building and tells her to be good and do whatever the teacher says. Zelda goes inside and stands with her back against the wall. So many children all laughing and talking in a strange language she does not understand. A woman in a brown skirt approaches Zelda. She says some funny sounding words. Zelda stares at her mouth. She says them again and Zelda strains her ears. One of the words is not unlike her name. She nods her head and the teacher steers her by the shoulders into a room full of tiny desks, a small child at each one. The children all stare at Zelda; they are half her size. The woman in the brown skirt leads Zelda to an empty desk in front. She sits and breathes in quickly to keep from crying out for the desk is too small and she has bumped her knee.

Another woman stands at the front of the classroom. She must be the teacher, Zelda thinks. The woman opens her mouth and strange sounds tumble out, one on top of the other and Zelda understands none of them. How will she ever learn this strange music? Zelda cannot even tell where one word stops and the next one begins. The morning drags on and Zelda tries not to fall asleep. All of a sudden, a very loud bell rings and all the children run out of the room. Zelda does not know what to do. Will they come back? Should she run away, too? Where did they go?

The teacher is still here. She says something to Zelda. Zelda smiles shyly and shakes her head. The teacher says something to Zelda again, only this time louder. Zelda feels a little frightened, maybe she did something wrong? Then the teacher holds up one finger and leaves the room. In a minute she is back with an older boy, a boy Zelda's age.

"Go home," the boy says in Yiddish. "It's time to go home." Zelda leaps up, so happy to hear the familiar sounds that she almost kisses the boy on her way out the door and back home to her momma.

Further suggestions: In the warm-up exercise on "firsts" you came up with a list of "firsts" that are common experience: first date, first sexual experience, first lie. Choose a character and describe these "firsts" for her. Also make a list of "firsts" particular to this character (i.e. the first night Zelda sleeps alone after Murray dies) and describe them as well.

Recommended reading: Leaving Brooklyn is a novel by Lynne Sharon Schwartz that goes into great detail about a young girl's first sexual experience.

I Remember

Assignment

(For related writing exercise, see page 26.) Even though your character starts to come alive the minute you begin to write about her, your character also has a personal history. Things have happened to her before you started writing about her. If for example, your story begins with a thirty-five year old character, that character has thirty-five years of experiences and memories behind her. This information is important for you to know, because your character's past shapes who she is today.

Choose a character and write down the words, "I remember." Now, writing in your character's voice, write down whatever comes into your mind. When that memory draws to a close, begin another one with the words, "I remember." In this manner, compile a list of your character's memories.

Example: Zelda's memories

I remember Ellis Island: holding tight to my mother's hand and so many people all talking at once but I couldn't understand what anyone was saying.

I remember my first day at school; sitting at a desk that was too small for me and everyone staring and saying strange words I couldn't understand.

I remember the first time I walked into the factory. The noise was so loud I thought my head would explode. I remember coming home from work: the fresh smell of the ocean air the minute I got off the subway and the rush to get home before dark.

I remember the smell of my mother's house every Friday night: chicken soup, fresh challah and Ajax.

I remember the first Shabbos I spent with Murray's family. So many people: aunts and uncles and cousins and brothers and sisters. And his mother and father, of course. It was so noisy compared to my house where there was just the two of us. I remember telling Murray's mother that, and the look of horror that crossed her face when she realized my mother was all alone on the Shabbos.

I remember our first apartment. It was in the basement and when I looked out the window all I saw was shoes.

I remember the first night I ever slept in the bed by myself. First I slept with my mother; we only had the one room, and then I slept with Murray, of course. The first night after he was gone I didn't sleep the whole night. I couldn't decide should I sleep on his side, should I sleep on my side, so I just lay there in the middle, like a little child, lost.

Further suggestions: Compile lists of "I remember's" for different characters and see what you learn about them. Also try writing a list of "I remember's" in one character's voice every day for a week. Add a word, such as "I remember dreaming," for a more focused list of memories (see page 28 for related writing exercise). Try expanding any of your character's memories (see page 29 for related writing exercise) and exaggerating them (see page 30 for related writing exercise).

Flashbacks

Assignment

Using flashbacks is a fiction writing technique that interweaves the past with the present. A character is in the present moment (whenever that happens to be in your story) and then flashes back to something that happened in the past. The memory should be significant and reveal something about the character.

How do you get your character out of the present into the past and back to the present again? Think about what causes you to remember something. Usually seeing, hearing, smelling, touching or tasting something that reminds you of a particular person, event or time in your life, will cause a memory to rise to the surface of your mind. For example, often when I water the plants in my apartment, the smell of the damp soil reminds me of the vegetable garden I had when I was twenty. The other day, I heard two people conversing in Hebrew and I was immediately reminded of the years I spent in Israel.

What brings a character back to the present moment? Again, a sight, sound, smell, texture or taste. If I am standing on a step ladder pouring water into a spider plant's soil, lost in a memory of weeding my garden, the sun hot on my bare shoulders, the sound of a ringing telephone, the feel of my hand going numb from holding the watering can, or the sight of water overflowing onto the floor will quickly bring me back to the present.

Choose a character and write a short scene where your character is in the present moment, then goes back in a memory of the past and then returns to the present.

Example:

Zelda is sitting on the boardwalk, the sun warm on her face, the bench hard against her bones. A soft wind blows through her hair and she squints against it. A cloud blocks out the sun for a minute, then passes and her face is warm again. The sun is too bright to look into, so she closes her eyes just like at the doctor's office last week when the doctor brought that lamp he pulls down from the ceiling closer so he could get a good look at her face. He'd said she shouldn't sit out in the sun no more, it's no good for her skin. The doctor was young and good-looking. Zelda had thought he'd make a nice husband for Deena, even if he wasn't too bright. After he'd finished going on about the sun and her skin, he'd told Zelda she should lose some weight, it was no good for her heart to carry around extra pounds. "Doctor," Zelda had said, "I ain't interested in no beauty contests at my age. Let me enjoy a piece of babka, an extra slice of challah once in a while, it wouldn't kill me." The doctor smiled and shook his head and Zelda shook her head now, remembering. The wind picked up again, and Zelda wrapped her coat around her body tighter, glad to have a little extra meat on her old bones.

Further suggestions: Practice writing scenes where your characters move from present to past to present. Use any of your characters' "I remember's" as the basis for a flashback.

Recommended reading: In the novel *Briar Rose*, by Jane Yolen, the protagonist, Becca, is searching for clues about her grandmother's life. Becca meets Josef P. who, in a brilliantly written, lengthy flashback, tells Becca everything she yearns to know.

Dreams

Assignment

(For related writing exercise, see page 25). Just as you must know your characters' memories, you must know their dreams as well. What is happening in the subconscious of your character's mind? Dreams can be very useful in a story. A dream can help a character remember something from the past, or prophesy something that will happen in the future. A dream can reveal a hidden fear or secret desire. Writing dreams can be very freeing and loads of fun, as dreams provide a great opportunity to use your imagination. Dreams don't have to make sense. In a dream two people who ordinarily would never meet can come face to face. In a dream, your character can be anywhere and do anything. Dreams can be creepy, magical, surreal, euphoric, erotic or realistic.

Choose a character and write down a dream she's had. The dream should reveal something about your character. Write the dream in the present tense as if it is happening right now.

Example: Zelda's dream

Zelda is standing on the boardwalk, leaning against the railing and tossing crusts of rye bread down to the seagulls below her on the beach. One seagull in particular is very aggressive. He swoops down and calls loudly, frightening the other birds away. "Go on, don't be so selfish," Zelda says, shaking a finger at him. The bird looks up and Zelda gasps, for the sea gull is wearing wire rimmed glasses just like Murray's. "Murray, is that you?" Zelda asks. Another bird is wearing tiny gold earrings just like the pair that belonged to Zelda's mother. A third gull has on a blue satin yarmulke, like Zelda's father-in-law, may he rest in peace.

Zelda flings the bread crumbs onto the beach. When the birds are done eating, they start to fly away. "Wait, wait, I'm coming with you," Zelda calls, flapping her arms. But she cannot fly. The birds flock into a formation of letters that spell out: NOT YET. Zelda's hands fly up to her chest in shock, then she waves to the birds until they are out of sight.

Further suggestions: Choose a character and write down her dreams every day for a week. Also try writing the following dreams for your character:

- happiest dream
- scariest dream
- silliest dream
- dream from childhood
- recurring nightmare
- saddest dream
- angriest dream
- sexiest dream
- recurring dream

Recommended reading: Anya, by Susan Fromberg Schaeffer, is a novel that begins and ends with the main character having a powerful dream.

All Alone

Assignment

An excellent way to get to know your character is to observe her alone. We all act differently when we are completely by ourselves; we let our hair down so to speak when there is no one else around we have to worry about impressing, or looking like a fool in front of. Often when we are alone we are the most vulnerable; our guard is down. So, too, with your characters.

Choose a character and describe that character in a private moment, when she is alone, doing something ordinary such as getting dressed in the morning or taking a bath. Use lots of sensory detail so that your writing comes alive and something about the character is revealed.

Example: Zelda taking a bath

Zelda runs the water in the tub and fastens a hair net around her head. My hair is so thin, she thinks as she tucks a stray end in. I used to have so much hair, a braid down my back thick as a man's arm. Zelda unzips her house dress, steps out of it and hangs it on a hook on the back of the door. She steadies herself with one hand on the rim of the tub and lifts her right foot, then her left into the warm water. "Oh, is that good," Zelda says as she kneels down and shuts the faucet. She lowers herself into the water, holding onto the rim carefully so her feet shouldn't fly out from under her, resulting in a broken hip, or God forbid, worse. Finally, Zelda is settled in the tub with her head resting on its ledge, the warm water seeping into her bones. Zelda sighs, grateful for the few small pleasures she has left in this life: a warm bath, a hot cup of tea.

Zelda reaches for the soap and moves it slowly along her body. First down her arm with the loose flesh hanging off her bones and then across her wrinkled breasts that fall to her waist. Zelda can no longer lift her legs so she just lets them soak as she scrubs her back with a rough brush. Zelda remembers how Murray used to scratch her back and how good that felt. And how he used to zip her up in the back and kiss the nape of her neck. Well, the scrub brush was as good as fingernails, and her house dress she could zip and unzip by herself if she wore it backwards with the zipper in front. As for the kiss, well, she was too old for that now anyway.

Zelda sits up and hoists herself out of the tub, the water making a sucking sound around her body. She dries off quickly, she shouldn't catch a cold or pneumonia, God forbid. She steps into her house dress, zips it up tight and pads off to the kitchen for her morning cup of tea.

Further suggestions: Make a list of everyday solitary activities and describe your character doing each one. Some suggestions are:

- taking a bath
- getting dressed in the morning
- getting ready for bed
- eating a meal alone
- going grocery shopping
- driving in the car
- walking in the woods
- sweeping the floor
- ironing
- doing the laundry
- looking in the mirror
- masturbating
- reading
- crying

Also try picking one activity and describe several different characters doing the same activity (for example, describe Susan getting dressed in the morning, Sarah getting dressed in the morning, Sam getting dressed in the morning, etc.).

Recommended reading: "Solitary Pleasure," a short story by Kitty Tsui from the book *Finding Courage,* edited by Irene Zahava, describes a character who spends several days alone in her apartment struggling with her alcoholism.

----- *Pleasures* -----

Assignment

(For related writing exercise, see page 35.) Choose a character and make a list of activities that character enjoys doing. Pick one activity and describe it, putting in as many sensory details as possible so that your reader feels the same pleasure your character does when participating in this activity.

Zelda's Pleasures

- cooking
- cleaning the apartment
- seeing a baby or a small child down on the Avenue or on the boardwalk
- talking to Deena on the phone or better yet having Deena over for a visit
- eating a good meal
- finding a good bargain
- bumping into someone on the Avenue and having a nice chat
- smelling the ocean air
- drinking a cup of hot tea and eating something sweet
- playing cards
- sitting on the boardwalk in the sun
- taking off her brassiere and girdle at night

Example: Zelda, sitting on the boardwalk

Zelda eased herself onto the wooden bench with a grateful "oy." It was a weekday so the boardwalk wasn't so crowded and she was glad to have a bench to herself. Sometimes she found herself sitting next to an old man sleeping with his mouth open making awful sounds, or a bunch of teenagers blaring that noise they called music and blowing smoke in her face.

She closed her eyes and took a deep breath, luxuriating in the fresh, ocean air. The only sounds she heard were the steady rhythm of the ocean rolling in and out against the beach; the sea gulls circling overhead calling; and the heels of an occasional person clicking against the boardwalk behind her. The sun felt warm on her face, like the promise of something good to come and Zelda felt all the aches and pains of her old body temporarily dissolve in the heat. She opened her eyes and looked out over the ocean. When I was young, Zelda mused, I never had a minute, always running here and there, never mind a whole afternoon to myself like this. Zelda closed her eyes again and settled against the bench for a nice long rest. Sometimes, like right now, she didn't mind being old.

Further suggestions: Go down the list of pleasures you compiled for your character and describe her doing each one.

Never Say "Never"

Assignment

In the previous writing exercise you got to know a character by writing about activities she has engaged in and found pleasure in. This exercise will give you the opportunity to get to know a character in a different way; you will be writing about a character doing something she has never done before and never had any intention of doing. Choose a character and make a list of things your character would never do. Then choose an item on the list and describe your character doing this activity in such a way that something about the character is revealed. Don't spend too much time trying to figure out why your character is doing something she swore she would never do. Just start writing, and assume that circumstances beyond your character's control have led her to this situation.

What Zelda would never do
- let her hair go gray
- not polish her nails
- leave the house without lipstick on
- get married again
- yell at Deena
- wear flat shoes
- steal
- commit murder
- eat a ham sandwich or a cheeseburger
- not go to synagogue on the High Holy Days
- go to bed without washing out her bloomers

Example: Zelda lets her hair go gray

Zelda stared at herself in the mirror. "Oy, who is that old woman in the glass," she asked herself, raising a hand to her hair. How could there be so much gray after missing just one week at the beauty parlor? Zelda had been afraid to go out last Wednesday in such a storm and the beauty parlor had been too busy to reschedule her before her next regular appointment. Thank God, tomorrow was already Wednesday again.

Zelda pulled her hair away from her face, staring at the wide gray streaks at her temples. Now I first look old, she thought, tears forming in her eyes. She blinked quickly, not daring to let them fall, for if she did, would they ever stop? So much lost over all the years: her mother, her father, all her brothers and sisters, for they were all at least twelve years older than Zelda, her husband, most of her neighbors, and of course, her youth.

"Foolish woman," Zelda shook her finger at herself in the glass. "At your age you should care what you look like? You think anybody's looking at you? Go on." But she did care. Always had and always would, even if she lived another eighty years, God forbid.

Zelda tied a scarf around her head and laughed at herself. "Now you look like a bride," she said, remembering the good old days when a new bride would cut off her hair and wear a scarf or a wig. Who would marry Zelda now? And would she even want a new husband at her age? No, not a new husband, Zelda thought, the same old husband I was used to. The one who would bring me a drink of water in the middle of the night, the one who would zip me up in the back when I couldn't reach, the one who would tell me, gray hair or not, you're still beautiful. Once again Zelda's eyes filled with tears and once again she forbade them to fall.

Further suggestions: Go down your list and describe your character doing each activity on it. Do this even if you are absolutely positive your character would never do these things. (Think about how many times in your life you've done something you swore you'd never do.) You will learn a lot about your character by observing how she handles these situations.

Rituals: Part 1

Assignment

All of us have rituals to help us organize our lives and give us a feeling of continuity and predictability. For example, what is your morning ritual? Do you shower, then dress, then drink your coffee, then blow dry your hair? What is your coming-home-after-work ritual? Do you check your answering machine and feed the cat, or do you read the paper and have a cup of tea?

In addition to daily rituals, there are weekly, monthly and yearly rituals. Perhaps on Tuesday nights you always watch a certain TV show. Or once a month you meet a certain friend for dinner. Or once a year you visit a loved one's grave.

Choose a character and make a list of her rituals. Describe one ritual in detail, so that something about the character is revealed.

Zelda's rituals

- takes a bath every morning
- watches Mike Douglas every afternoon
- lights Shabbos candles every Friday night
- speaks to Deena on the phone every Monday, Thursday and Saturday
- takes a walk on the boardwalk every day
- goes shopping on the Avenue every afternoon
- drinks a cup of tea and eats something sweet every evening
- washes out her undergarments every evening
- spends every Passover with her daughter's family
- goes to synagogue every year on the High Holy Days

Example: <u>Zelda, lighting the Shabbos candles</u>

It is Friday night. The sun has gone down and there is a hazy glow outside Zelda's kitchen window. It is time to draw the curtains, tuck herself in for the night and light the Shabbos candles.

Zelda opens the kitchen cabinet and gets two fat, white candles out of the box. She fits them into the silver candlesticks that belonged to her mother and always stand erect on her kitchen table. Then she goes into her bedroom for the bit of lace she always places on her head to say the prayer. She keeps the lace in her night table drawer next to Murray's blue velvet yarmulke, the one he used to pin to his wavy gray hair on the High Holy Days when he went to synagogue.

Zelda sighs as she recrosses the apartment and goes back into the kitchen. She still isn't used to lighting the candles alone. After the prayer, when Murray was alive, he would say, "Shabbot Shalom," and kiss her before he sat down at his place, waiting for the soup to be served. Now there's no one to kiss and no one to serve. But still, a tradition is a tradition.

Zelda strikes a match and lights the two candles. She makes three circles with her hands and then puts her fingertips over her eyes as she says the blessing. Though Zelda is not a religious woman, she does find comfort in carrying on a ritual she had mostly indulged in for Murray's sake. After she recites the ancient Hebrew words, she opens her eyes and stares at the twin flames before her. Everything comes in pairs, Zelda thinks, not for the first time. Two candlesticks, two kitchen chairs, two sides of the bed... She removes her head covering and lays it out on the table beside the candles, then ladles out a bowl of soup for herself and sits down to eat.

Further suggestions: Go down your list and describe each of your character's rituals in detail, so that something about the character is revealed.

Recommended reading: In my own short story, "Only a Phase," from *A Letter To Harvey Milk,* two characters' daily rituals are described: a housewife's daily routine from morning until her husband comes home from work; and the woman's daughter, from the time she comes home from work until supper.

Rituals: Part II

Assignment

In writing about a character's ritual, we learn how she behaves in a predictable situation. She has performed this ritual before; it is always the same. But what happens when something unexpected occurs, making it impossible for the ritual to be carried out? Now you have the opportunity to learn about your character in an unfamiliar and unpredictable situation.

Using the ritual you wrote about in the last exercise, make a list of everything that might prevent your character from performing this ritual. Choose one such disturbance and write a scene in which your character starts to perform her ritual and then is unable to. How does your character respond to this unexpected situation? What do you learn about her?

Zelda, unable to light the Shabbos candles
- she ran out of candles
- she ran out of matches
- she fell asleep in the middle of the afternoon and didn't wake up until the next morning
- she forgot it was Friday
- she misplaced the candlesticks
- the candlesticks were stolen
- she is distracted by some emergency: a fire in the building or a neighbor calling for help
- she decides she doesn't believe in the ritual anymore
- she is away for the weekend and forgets to bring candles and candlesticks with her

Example:

It is Friday night and time for Zelda to light the candles. She opens the cabinet doors and reaches into the box for two fat, white candles, but her fingers don't find any. How can that be? Zelda squats down on her old, noisy knees and pulls out the box. It's definitely empty. Zelda scolds herself: how could you let this happen?

Zelda fishes around the rest of the cabinet among the pots and pans, hoping to find a candle that somehow fell out of the box and rolled into a corner. But she finds nothing.

Now what? Zelda peers out the window. It is already growing dark: the only light down below comes from the headlights of a double-parked car. I could run to the corner store, Zelda thinks and then almost laughs out loud. "With these legs, you think I can run?" she asks herself. Zelda stands up with her hands on her hips. No, it's too dangerous to go out on a Friday night by herself. The neighborhood wasn't what it used to be. If Murray was alive, she'd send him down.

Or, if Murray was alive, she wouldn't be afraid, they could go down together. If Murray this, if Murray that . . . Zelda shakes her head, trying to clear from it the great *if* of her life. Maybe I should knock on Doris' door, Zelda thinks. Maybe she has some candles. Zelda starts for the door and then stops. She really didn't want to get involved in a long conversation with Doris about whatever or more likely whoever was on Doris' mind.

Zelda comes back into the kitchen and looks at the empty candlesticks. Would it be so terrible to skip one Friday night? Unfortunately, the answer is yes. Zelda ransacks the kitchen and then moves into the living room. Maybe, just maybe, she had some candles tucked away somewhere.

When the living room is exhausted, Zelda moves into the bedroom. After Zelda searches through her things, she turns toward Murray's dresser and hesitates. She hasn't opened these drawers for a whole year; is this the right time?

"There ain't no candles in there," Zelda says aloud, but that was beside the point. Zelda pulls open a drawer and steps back, then rushes forward to gather up the pile of white undershirts she finds there. They are so soft, so clean, so . . . so Murray. Zelda buries her face in the cloth and sobs for the first time since Murray died. She didn't even cry at the funeral.

But who would expect his clothes to smell just like him a whole year later? That familiar smell of soap, sweat, after-shave and onions. Zelda piles all Murray's clothes on top of the bed, lifting each garment to her face one last time. It was time to let go. Someone can use these shirts, these pants, these socks. It was time to let go of the past. Sunday, Zelda would call the synagogue and have them pick up Murray's things. They would know which charity was the neediest. And tomorrow she would buy herself a box of Shabbos candles, maybe two boxes to be safe. But tonight, she would sleep in the dark, without the light from the Shabbos candles flickering in the kitchen, with all Murray's clothes surrounding her, alone.

Further suggestions: Try disrupting your character's ritual with different items on your list, and see how she responds to the various, unpredictable situations she finds herself in.

5

Monologues: Listening In

In a monologue, the narrator (the person telling the story) and the main character are one and the same. In other words, the main character tells the story in her own voice, using the first person pronoun, "I," when referring to herself. Writing a monologue in your character's voice gives you the opportunity to get inside your character's mind and see the world through her eyes. It also allows you to develop your character's voice; you actually "hear" your character speaking.

When writing a monologue, there is something called the "implied you." Since a character is speaking, it is assumed the character is speaking to someone. That someone can be a specific person or that someone can be what is known as the "general you" or no one in particular. In this section of writing exercises, we will practice writing both kinds of monologues.

Postcards

Assignment

Remember the expression, "a picture is worth a thousand words"? Find a postcard of a character who intrigues you and write a monologue in that character's voice (see if you can go for a thousand words). Don't plan what the character is going to say; just let the words pour out in a stream-of-consciousness manner. Your character should not be addressing anyone in particular.

Example: Fashion model in a bikini top and mini-skirt, strolling up the beach

"You think I have an easy, glamorous life, right? All I have to do is smile and say cheese and the whole world falls at my feet. Well, that's a bunch of lies, big time. Don't you believe it for a minute. Modeling is hell and I can't wait to quit. Quit, ha, that's a laugh. They throw you out of the business when you get too old, like twenty-two or twenty-three. I've got a year left tops, before I'm all washed up. But I don't care. The first thing I'm gonna do when I get out of here is eat a cheeseburger. Maybe even two. With french fries and a chocolate shake. Now that would be heaven. You wanna know what I ate yesterday? One tossed green salad with low calorie Italian dressing. That's it. Oh, except for about eight hundred cups of black coffee. What, you think women are born looking like this? Ask Cher, it takes a lot of work to stay this thin. Some of the girls eat whatever they want and puke it up afterwards but that's too disgusting; I'd rather not eat. I'm sure you're wondering about my boobs. I paid for those of course, everyone does. That's one thing about this job: the money's fantastic. Why else do you think we stick it out, for our health? Ha, that's a joke. We're all either bulimic or anorexic or . . . whoops, I gotta go. They're calling me for a shoot. Time to smile now. Cheese."

Further suggestions: Collect a bunch of postcards and practice writing stream-of-consciousness monologues in different character's voices. Try women, men, old people, children, people of various ethnic groups, celebrities, etc.

What's in a Name?

Assignment

Sometimes all we know about a person is their name, yet often we form an opinion of them based on just that information. Open the phone book and write down the first name your eye falls upon. Write a stream-of-consciousness monologue in this character's voice.

Example: Mark Irving

"My name is Mark Irving but my friends call me Irving Mark. I don't know why, really. It started in junior high, when we all ranked on each other for any reason we could think of. If a guy had lots of pimples we'd call him 'zithead' or if a guy was fat we'd call him 'lardo.' You know, that's just how guys are at that age. So, there wasn't too much wrong with me except this weird name made of two first names. Mark is okay, but Irving? I'm not even Jewish. So my friends started calling me Irving Mark and then they started calling me Question Mark and Exclamation Mark. When I went off to college, every single professor would ask me on the first day of class, 'Is it Mark Irving or Irving Mark?' At one point I considered changing my name to Irving Marks but I never did.

"Now I'm getting married and my new name is going to be Mark Irving-Goodperson. Can you believe it? See, my fiancé, Nancy, changed her name from Goodman to Goodperson years ago because she's kind of a feminist and didn't want a man in her name. And, before we got engaged, we had to have all these discussions because she didn't want to have a man's first name as her last name. I thought about giving Irving up and just being Mark Goodperson but I don't know, I just couldn't give up my name after all these years. 'How do you think women feel?' Nancy asked me. She's determined to make me a feminist.

"Well, then we thought we'd each keep our own last names, but that could be confusing for the kids, which I want ten of, at least. So, we compromised, which is what marriage is all about I'm told (Nancy wants three kids so I guess we'll have six and a half). So soon I won't be Mark Irving anymore, I'll be a nerd with a hyphenated name. Oh well, that's the way it goes."

Further suggestions: Choose a different name from the phone book every day for a week and practice writing stream-of-consciousness monologues in each character's voice.

Recommended reading: "Alan Allen," by Irene Zahava from *Word of Mouth, Volume Two,* edited by Irene Zahava, is a monologue in the voice of an adolescent girl. "Mrs. Saunders Writes Her Name To The World," by Lynne Sharon Schwartz from her book *Acquainted With The Night,* is a short story that revolves around a character's name.

Perfect Strangers

Assignment

Go somewhere where you are sure to be around people you don't know: a bus station, restaurant, shopping mall or street corner. Write a stream-of-consciousness monologue in the voice of the first person you see.

Example: <u>Woman in shopping mall wearing fur coat</u>

"Listen, I'll tell you right now, I have as much right as anyone else to wear whatever the hell I want. The first punk that spills ketchup on this coat isn't going to recognize his own face in the mirror. Don't get me wrong, I'm a very nice person, but if someone's nasty to me, watch out. Don't bust my chops, if you know what I mean. That girl that just yelled 'Murderer!' at me, the attractive young lady with the purple hair and nose ring? She's wearing a leather jacket, for Chrissakes. So go figure. You know, the most aggressive people I've ever met in my life are vegetarians. Really. They've done studies, you know. On rats, which I think is quite appropriate. See, they starve them and see how their behavior changes. I hear they get pretty nasty. Hell, I'd get nasty if I was hungry all the time and that's the trouble with these crazy vegetarians. They don't get enough protein, see, so they really can't be held responsible for their actions.

"This is the last time I'm going to say it. I worked damn hard for this coat, it's frigging freezing outside and I have the right to be warm and look fabulous. You have a problem with that, you can just stick it where the sun don't shine."

Further suggestions: Every day for a week, write a stream-of-consciousness monologue in the voice of the first stranger you encounter in your day.

Recommended reading: "Route 23: 10th and Bigler to Bethlehem Pike," by Becky Birtha from her book *Lovers' Choice*, is a complete short story told as a monologue in the voice of a woman on a bus.

Speaking of Bodies

Assignment

(For related writing exercise, see page 74.) For the remaining exercises on monologue, choose a character or characters you are interested in developing.

In the section on character, we have written about what a character's body looks like; now we will practice writing about what a character's body feels like. Pick a part of the body and write a monologue about that body part in your character's voice. Write in stream-of-consciousness style and see where the monologue takes you.

Example: <u>Zelda, speaking about her arms</u>

"My arms, feh, look how the skin hangs off my bones. I can't believe it, so strong my arms used to be, just like a man's. I don't wear short sleeves no more, it ain't nice to see an old lady's arms flapping in the breeze with so many old age spots it looks like I'm wearing polka dots.

"So that's the way it is, but I ain't complaining. I'm eighty years old and I still do all my own shopping and cooking and cleaning, so I guess I got some strength in these arms yet. You know, I still do exercises at night to firm up my arms, I'll show you, I learned from Jack LaLanne. He ain't on no more, it's a pity, he had a really good program. Now they got all these skinny girls jumping around, it makes me dizzy just to watch them. And so skinny they are, oy, I'm afraid they shouldn't faint, right on the television.

"Years ago, if a girl was so skinny, a boy wouldn't look twice at her. When I was young, boys wanted a girl who had a little shape to her, not someone who looked like a stick. I had some figure then, let me tell you, I haven't always been an old lady. But everything's different now, never mind.

"Look, I still remember from Jack LaLanne, I'll show you. You put your arms up and you make circles, see, first little ones, then big ones, to the front and then to the back, like this. Not bad for an old lady, huh? Now I'm tired already, come, let's take a little rest."

Further suggestions: Choose a character and write monologues in that character's voice in which she talks about different parts of her body. Try writing about your character's:

- arms
- hands
- ears
- mouth
- back
- breasts

- legs
- feet
- nose
- shoulders
- belly
- neck

Recommended reading: "Bodies," by Patricia Roth Schwartz, from her book *The Names of the Moons of Mars*, is a short story told as a monologue in which the narrator talks about the bodies of others as well as her own.

I Wish

Assignment

Knowing what your character desires is important because our desires are what motivate us. Choose a character and write a stream-of-consciousness monologue in that character's voice, starting with the words, "I wish . . ."

Example (told in Zelda's voice)

"I wish I could speak good English. I came here when I was six but still after seventy-four years, I don't talk good. I wish my mother and father was still alive, I ain't got no one to talk Jewish to except Sophie and I'm mad on her, she cheats at cards all the time. I wish I was young again and I knew then what I know now. I wish Deena would get married already, twenty-two isn't so old yet, maybe she's twenty-three already, I don't remember, but if she doesn't watch out, she'll wind up an old maid. I wish Murray was still alive, of course, so I would have someone to talk to besides the furniture. I wish everything didn't hurt me so much, my hands, my feet, but I ain't gonna complain, who's gonna hear me anyway, God? I wish the winter wasn't so cold and the summer wasn't so hot and where does this wishing get me? It's foolish to wish for things, wishing don't change anything. You gotta work hard and make the best of what you got and keep your troubles to yourself, and that's all."

Further suggestions: Practice writing monologues that start with the words "I wish" for different characters. Also try:

"I want . . ."
"I don't want . . ."
"I always . . ."
"I never . . ."
"Let me explain . . ."

Recommended reading: *Weetzie Bat*, by Francesca Lia Block, is a truly delightful novel in which a character's three wishes unexpectedly come true.

First Impressions

Assignment

In the previous exercises on monologue, your characters weren't speaking to anyone in particular; they were speaking to the "general you." In the next two exercises, we will practice writing monologues in which your character is talking to someone in particular.

Choose a character and write a monologue in which that character is speaking to someone they are just meeting for the first time. Start the monologue with the words, "The first thing I want you to know about me is . . ."

Example: <u>Zelda, addressing her new neighbor, Stephanie</u>

"The first thing I want you to know about me is I'm very independent. I never ask nobody for nothing, so you don't have to worry, I ain't gonna bother you. You'll like it here, it's a nice neighborhood. I can tell you where the best butcher is and who has the freshest vegetables. I been here a long time. Some people my age move down to Florida, but not me, I like it here. I don't even go down for the winter, like some people do. Sophie, you know Sophie down the hall? You'll meet her, I'll take you over, I'll introduce you. Anyway, every time I turn around, Sophie's packing or unpacking. That ain't no way to live. I like to stay in one place.

"I know everyone in the building and everyone knows me. They got a problem, they come talk to Zelda. You too, darling, feel free. I know you're young, you got better things to do than have a cup of coffee with an old lady, but come any time. And if my TV's too loud, just give a holler, I'll turn it down. The walls here are thin, like paper. The couple that lived here before you, I heard them yelling and screaming all the time. And other things, too, but never mind, you're too young for that.

"All right, I'll let you get settled, but give a call if you need anything. Or just if you feel lonely. Believe me, I know what it's like to be all alone and you're too young to suffer like that. It was nice to meet you, darling. I'm sure we'll get along just fine, there's nothing like a good neighbor. All right now, bye-bye."

Further suggestions: Write monologues in different characters' voices starting with the phrase, "The first thing I want you to know about me is . . ." Make sure your character is speaking to a specific person.

Recommended reading: My own story, "Right Off The Bat," from *Secrets,* is a monologue in the voice of a twelve year old girl that starts with this phrase.

What I Could Never Tell You

Assignment

All characters have secrets; things they would never tell anyone. Think of the secrets you hold dear and what they reveal about you. Your characters have secrets, too, and your job as a writer is to learn these secrets in order to understand your character fully.

Choose a character and write a monologue in that character's voice in which she addresses a specific person. Start the monologue with the words, "I could never tell you . . ."

Example: <u>Zelda, speaking to her granddaughter, Deena</u>

"I could never tell you what happened in the old country, shah now, don't even ask me, you're too sensitive to know about such things. I remember when you was a baby and we were in the car; you would cry over every squirrel we passed that got run over. You can't be like that in this world. You gotta be strong. Anyway, you shouldn't know from such things; it's over, forget about it. I could never tell you how much everything hurts me, my arms, my legs, my back, my feet. You would only worry, and I want you should just enjoy. I could never tell you how much I love you because no matter how hard I try, even after being in this country seventy-four years, still, I don't talk so good, I still don't know how to say it. Americans love everything, they love this movie, that movie, they love a candy bar, a pair of shoes, love, love, love, how can the same word possibly say what I feel in my heart for you? So I tell you in Jewish, *ich hob dire libe* and that darling, Deena, you don't understand."

Further suggestions: Make a list of all the important people in your character's life. Write a monologue in your character's voice to each person on the list, starting with the words, "I could never tell you . . ." Include (when appropriate) your character's:

• mother	• spouse or lover
• father	• ex-lover
• siblings	• potential lover
• children	• boss

- grandchildren
- best friend
- rival
- teacher
- co-worker
- neighbor

Recommended reading: In my own story, "A Letter To Harvey Milk," from the book by the same title, one character tells another a story he's never told anyone and this affects both characters very deeply.

Dear Diary

Assignment

Writing a diary or journal in a character's voice is another way to practice writing monologues. Here, your character is not addressing anyone in particular; she is recording her thoughts and feelings on paper. If you've ever kept a diary, you know it's a safe place to write down your most private thoughts and feelings; things you might not tell another living soul. This is what your character will write in her diary, too.

Choose a character and write a diary entry in her voice. Do this even if your character is not the type of person who would write in a diary.

Example: <u>Zelda's diary</u>

Dear Diary,

Today I was down on the Avenue and who did I see but Doris. I didn't even know she was back from Florida yet. Maybe Sophie will be back soon, too.

Doris is very tan, but just between you, me and the lamppost, she looks terrible. Of course I would never tell her that—I told her she looks terrific—but the sun is too strong down there, her face looks like a piece of shoe leather. But if you don't have nothing nice to say, don't say nothing. You know it ain't necessary to hurt a person's feelings.

Years ago, I saw some cocktail napkins in a joke store, and they said on them, "If you don't have anything nice to say, sit next to me." I could give those napkins to a few people and it wouldn't be no joke, believe me. Like Doris, for instance. She had to make a comment about everybody in the building: this one looks terrible, that one got so fat. I wonder what she says behind my back. All right, never mind, I'm glad she's back, all in one piece. Even if I don't like her so much, there ain't so many of us left, I'm glad I got one more person I can talk to.

So, that's all. In five minutes the rice will be done and I'll eat a little and watch TV and go to bed. If God wills it, I'll live another day and write a little more tomorrow.

Further suggestions: Keep a diary in your character's voice for a week, a month or even longer. This is an excellent way to get to know a character from the inside out.

Recommended reading: The Diary of a Young Girl, by Anne Frank, is an actual diary of a young girl in hiding during World War II that reads like a compelling piece of fiction. *As We Are Now,* by May Sarton, is a fictitious monologue supposedly written on scraps of paper by an old woman in a nursing home. "The Notebooks of Leni Clare," by Sandy Boucher from her book by the same name, is a short story that interweaves excerpts from the main character's diary throughout the narrative.

Letters

Assignment

When writing letters, your character is addressing a specific person. She will probably not reveal her deepest secrets like she does when writing in a diary that isn't meant to be read by anyone. Yet, often we write very personal things in letters, for it is sometimes easier to share things on paper than it is face to face.

Choose a character and write a letter in her voice to someone specific.

Example: <u>Zelda, writing a note to her new neighbor</u>

Dear Stephanie,

I'm sorry to bother you, darling, that's why I'm writing you this note instead of knocking on your door, maybe you got company or something, I don't know. Not that you'd hear me knocking anyway with all that noise you call music going on in there.

Stephanie, darling, please, do you think you could turn down your Victrola once in a while? First of all I'm worried you shouldn't go deaf. If I can hear your music through the walls with my lousy ears, inside your house must be like a rocket ship. I'm afraid you're gonna wind up with a busted ear drum or worse.

And second of all, darling, I need some sleep. I don't want to make no trouble for you, Stephanie, you're a nice girl, you always offer to carry one of my bags when I meet you on the stairs, and I appreciate that, believe me. But maybe you could turn it down a little bit at night so I can get some sleep? What can I tell you, even at my age, a girl needs her beauty rest. Thank you, darling.

Your neighbor,
Zelda

Further suggestions: Try writing different letters in your character's voice. Write a letter to any of the important people in her life from the list you wrote (see page 113). Write their replies, as well. Also try:

- a business letter
- a love letter
- a threatening letter
- a letter of apology
- a letter of complaint
- a fan letter

You can also invent a pen pal for your character and write their correspondence.

Recommended reading: Of course the classic example of a book written in the form of letters is *The Color Purple*, by Alice Walker. *Prisoners*, a novel by Dorothy Bryant, begins with the correspondence of a man in jail and a woman "on the outside." *The Kryptonite Kid*, by Joseph Torchia, is a novel told completely in letters from a young boy to Superman.

6

Dialogue: Let's Talk About It

When writing dialogue, the rule of thumb to remember is this: good dialogue speaks; poor dialogue reads. In other words, you want your reader to feel like she is listening in on a conversation, not reading words on a page when she gets to the dialogue in your story.

An important means to this end is keeping your characters' voices alive and distinct from one another. Let your characters speak for themselves; don't put words in their mouths and make them sound like you think they should sound. For example, Zelda, the character I've been working with, does not speak correct English. She often inverts the words of a sentence: "So strong my arms used to be," instead of "My arms used to be so strong." If I forced Zelda to speak correct English, her dialogue would sound forced and I would lose the character's integrity.

On the other hand, Mark Irving, the character I invented earlier when working with monologue, would never invert his sentences. And he uses slang expressions such as "zit-head" that Zelda would never use. Each character's use of language is unique.

Writing dialogue is tricky because when you read good dialogue it is easy to think the author just wrote down exactly what she heard, and that was that. Not so. The author achieved that "natural effect" by putting a lot of thought and hard work into the writing, as you will soon see.

In the days ahead while we are focusing on dialogue, be aware of the conversations you participate in and the conversations going on around you. Notice how people talk to each other, interrupt each other, ignore each other, talk over each other. The following exercises will teach you how to portray all this in writing.

"I, Object..."

Assignment

Just for the fun of it and as a warm-up, write a dialogue between two inanimate objects. Write your dialogue in the form of a play, without a narrator; this helps keep the focus on what is being said.

Example: Gold earrings and silver earrings

GOLD: God, I hope she picks me today. I'm going stir crazy in this jewelry box.

SILVER: I hope I get to stay here all day and rest. Yesterday was hell.

GOLD: What happened?

SILVER: First of all, when she was putting me on in the morning, she dropped me right in the toilet

GOLD: Gross!

SILVER: I'll say. Then, when she got to work she took off her coat and got me all tangled up in her scarf.

GOLD: You look a little bent out of shape.

SILVER: I am, believe me.

GOLD: Still, you get to go places, see things . . .

SILVER: Not really. I mean I can't see much under all that hair of hers. And no one can see me. I don't know why she bothers. She might as well keep me in her pocket.

GOLD: Really? The one time I got to go out, her hair was all up in a French twist and I got to see everything.

SILVER: You don't say. Gee, maybe she's ashamed of me.

GOLD: Then why would she pick you all the time?

SILVER: Beats me.

GOLD: I can't help but think I did something wrong that night because she's never picked me again.

SILVER: She has nothing to be ashamed of. I'm as good as gold.

GOLD: Sure you are. You know they say every cloud has a silver lining. They don't say every cloud has a gold lining. You think there's something wrong with me?

SILVER: Of course not. Well, here she comes. Maybe you'll get lucky this time.

GOLD: I hope so. If I don't get out of here soon, I'm going to tarnish.

Further suggestions: Practice writing the following:

- a dialogue between two related inanimate objects (i.e., a knife and fork, pen and paper, etc.)
- a dialogue between two inanimate objects not likely to meet (i.e., a microwave oven and a chain saw)
- a dialogue between two animals
- a dialogue between a person and an animal
- a dialogue between a person and an object
- a dialogue between an animal and an object

Recommended reading: Alice Notley has written a very funny dialogue called "Elephant and Ocean," in her book *Waltzing Matilda*. And in the book, *Fabulous Nobodies: A Novel About A Girl In Love with Her Clothes*, by Lee Tulloch, the narrator's "frocks" as she calls them, speak to her and to each other.

Eavesdropping

Assignment

Put on a trench coat and a pair of dark sunglasses and go some-where where you can listen in on two people talking. Record their conversation as you are hearing it, again in the form of a play with-out a narrator.

Example: Two women in a dressing room

#1: I don't know. I think this makes me look fat.

#2: It doesn't make you look fat. You look terrific.

#1: What about this?

#2: That's nothing. Are you taking this?

#1: No.

#2: What about this?

#1: No. That looked awful.

#2: Where's the hanger? Oh, here it is.

#1: Are you sure?

#2: It's you. C'mon, I gotta get home by 4:00.

#1: By 4:00? It's already 3:30.

#2: I know. Come on.

#1: What about the back?

#2: The back looks fine.

#1: Look at this.

#2: You can put a belt over that, no one will see it. I'm taking these out. Hurry up, okay?

#1: I can't decide.

Further suggestions: Every day for a week, eavesdrop and record the various conversations that you hear. Try writing down the conver-sation as you hear it. Also try not writing as you listen; instead try to recreate the dialogue an hour later. Then try a day later, and then a week later. Notice how the factor of time changes your writing.

Assignment

So far we have used imagination, observation skills and short term memory to practice writing dialogue. Now we will call on our long term memory as a resource. Write down a dialogue from your childhood that you participated in. Write it in play form, without a narrator .

Example: <u>Myself and my cousin, Ellen</u>

ELLEN: C'mon, Lesléa, I'll show you how to put on makeup.

LESLÉA: Why do you wear makeup?

ELLEN: To look pretty.

LESLÉA: Why do you want to look pretty?

ELLEN: So boys will like me.

LESLÉA: Why do you want boys to like you?

ELLEN: So I can get a boyfriend.

LESLÉA: Why do you want a boyfriend?

ELLEN: So I can get married.

LESLÉA: Why do you want to get married?

ELLEN: So I can have a baby.

LESLÉA: How do you have a baby?

ELLEN: You sleep with your husband and then you get pregnant and then you have the baby.

LESLÉA: How?

ELLEN: You just do.

LESLÉA: So, if you don't sleep with your husband, you can't have a baby?

ELLEN: No.

LESLÉA: Hooray! I'm never sleeping with my husband, I'm never having a baby. Never, never, never, never, never!

ELLEN: You're crazy.

Further suggestions: Write down a dialogue from your childhood every day for a week. Try dialogues from when you were very young up to dialogues from your teenage years. Try dialogues between yourself and other kids, and between yourself and adults.

Recommended reading: Allegra Maud Goldman, by Edith Konecky, is a wonderful novel told in the voice of a witty and intelligent girl on the brink of adolescence. Allegra has many amusing dialogues with various characters including her parents, her brother, several other relatives and a multitude of friends.

Thought/Action/Speech

Assignment

Up to now we have focused on speech: what people say to each other. However, fictional dialogue is much more than that: it is actually a combination of thought, action and speech. While two characters are having a conversation, a lot more than talking is going on. Each character is thinking and moving and there are things happening in the environment around them as well.

In life, all these things happen simultaneously. For example, while I am in a writing workshop answering a student's question, I am speaking and at the same time, I am searching my brain for an example to illustrate my point and scratching my left cheek. While all this is happening, one student coughs, another rummages through her purse and a third is taking notes. Of course, I don't know what any of them are thinking. And on top of all this, the hands on the wall clock are moving, someone is revving up a motorcycle outside the window and the sun has ducked behind a cloud, casting the room in shadow for a minute before it emerges again.

In life, all this happens at the same time. In writing, this is expressed as a series of events. Writing is linear: one word follows the next; they can't be piled one upon the other. Also, in writing, you get to choose which items are important enough to record and which can be left out (wouldn't it be great to have such power in real life!). Thus, in a story, in addition to choosing which details to leave in and which to take out, you are also constantly deciding on the order of things. Even though everything is happening at once, you choose to first write down what is being said, and then follow that with an action, then a thought, then another fragment of speech, then another action, etc.

We will practice writing dialogue by breaking it down into the three components of thought, action and speech. To do this, go back to the previous assignment, and choose a dialogue you wrote from your childhood. You've already written what the characters say to one another; that is the speech component. Now, write a summary of the characters' actions. This is the equivalent of stage directions in a play. You need only write an overview; the actions can be further developed when you weave them into the speech. For an example I will work with the dialogue I wrote for the previous exercise, between myself and my cousin Ellen.

Example: Action

I walk past Ellen's room and enter. She is sitting at a dressing table, looking in the mirror and applying makeup to her face: blush, eye shadow, mascara. I watch her and examine her makeup. She concentrates on what she is doing, though every once in a while she does look at me. At the end of our conversation, I climb up on the bed and start jumping up and down.

Two down and one to go. Now write a summary of your thoughts during this conversation. This is called an internal monologue. Since the story is being told from your point of view, you don't have to worry about what the other person is thinking; as you have no way of knowing that (we will discuss point of view in the next chapter).

Example: Thought

I wonder why Ellen puts all that junk on her face. I wonder why she likes boys so much. I hate boys, especially Mitchell. He always teases me. I wonder if Ellen will really get married. I wonder why anybody wants to. Then you have to cook and clean and you never have any fun. And then you have to have a baby. I don't want one, but I do wonder how you get one inside you. No one ever tells me when I ask. I want to know how it happens, so I can make sure it never happens to me.

Now weave the three components of thought, action and speech together into a fully developed dialogue.

Example: Thought/Action/Speech

My cousin Ellen is putting on her makeup. She does this everyday and it takes at least an hour. I don't know what the big deal is. She looks fine without it.

"C'mon, Lesléa. I'll show you how to put on some makeup," Ellen says, as I pass her door.

I go in and watch her for a minute. She is patting a big powder puff on her face.

"Why do you wear makeup?" I ask, picking up a tube of lipstick and opening it. It's red, like a stop sign.

"To look pretty." Ellen picks up a compact and opens it. She takes out a little brush and sweeps some blush up her cheeks.

"Why do you want to look pretty?" I open another tube of lipstick. This one's light pink.

"So boys will like me."

"Why do you want boys to like you?" Ellen's answer puzzles me. Boys are stupid. All they do is pull your hair and tease you, especially Mitchell who's in my class and always calls me frizzbomb.

"So I can get a boyfriend." Ellen brushes some blue stuff on her eyes.

"Why do you want a boyfriend?" I ask, since it's the last thing I would ever want.

"So I can get married."

I change my mind. Getting married is the last thing I would ever want. Then you have to cook and clean and you never have any fun. "Why do you want to get married?" I ask Ellen's reflection in the mirror.

She looks at me like I'm really stupid. "So I can have a baby."

I put down the mascara I am toying with, as this is a subject that's been on my mind lately. "How do you have a baby?"

"You sleep with your husband and then you get pregnant and then you have the baby."

" How? "

"You just do." Ellen outlines her lips with a tiny brush and then fills the lipstick in. I stare at her mouth.

"So, if you don't sleep with your husband you can't have a baby?"

"No."

"Hooray!" I climb up on Ellen's bed and start jumping up and down, thrilled with this new knowledge. "I'm never sleeping with my husband, I'm never having a baby," I shout. "Never, never, never, never, never!"

Ellen turns from the mirror and looks at me. "You're crazy," she says.

Further suggestions: Practice writing dialogues in this fashion of breaking the dialogue down into thought/action/speech every day for a week. You may use any of the dialogues you've written so far, or try writing some new ones.

Nuts and Bolts

Before we continue practicing dialogues, let us discuss the actual writing of dialogue. The first thing you must know is that everything contained in quotation marks is assumed to be spoken out loud by a character. The second thing to remember is that every time a new character speaks, you begin a new paragraph.

Thirdly, let's look at the words surrounding your characters' speech. A simple, "she said," or "he asked" is much more effective than a grandiose, "she interrogated," or "he explicated." These words draw unnecessary attention to themselves and distract your reader from what your characters are actually saying. Simple phrases such as "she said," fade into the background, which is where they belong.

As we've already discussed, dialogue is a combination of thought, action and speech. It is good to vary the order in which these three components occur, in order to keep your dialogue interesting.

Following are some examples of different ways to write dialogue.

"Don't yell at me," she said, putting up her hands as if to ward off a blow.
(speech, followed by who is speaking, followed by action)

She said, "Don't yell at me," and put up her hands as if to ward off a blow.
(who is speaking, followed by speech, followed by action)

She put up her hands as if to ward off a blow. "Don't yell at me," she said.
(action, followed by speech, followed by who is speaking)

Putting up her hands as if to ward off a blow, she said, "Don't yell at me."
(action, followed by who is speaking, followed by speech)

A fragment of speech can be interrupted by a thought or action as well:

"If you want someone to do the job right," she said, considering the options, "my advice is to hire a woman."
(speech, interrupted by who is speaking, followed by thought, followed by remainder of speech)

"If you want someone to do the job right," she considered the options, "my advice is to hire a woman."
(same as the previous example except that the word said, *though implied, is omitted)*

Notice that the above two examples are all one sentence. The example below, however, is three separate sentences.

"I love lasagna." She licked her lips in anticipation. "Do you think we should order some wine?"
(speech, followed by action, followed by speech)

Sometimes dialogue can be contained within dialogue. This can get a little tricky. When a character is directly quoting someone, use single quotes within quotation marks.

"So she said to me, 'What are you doing?' " Marla said. "And I answered, 'Oh nothing, Mom.' "
(speech containing direct quote, followed by who is speaking, followed by remainder of speech containing direct quote)

However, if a character is paraphrasing what someone has said and not quoting directly, single quotes are not used:

"So she asked me what I was doing," Marla said, "and I told her I wasn't doing anything."
(speech followed by who is speaking, followed by remainder of speech)

You can use a combination of these techniques as well:

"So she said to me, 'What are you doing?' " Marla said, "and I told her I wasn't doing anything."
(speech containing direct quote, followed by who is speaking, followed by remainder of speech with no direct quote)

And finally, you can have quite a bit of running dialogue without referring to who is speaking:

"Wanna go swimming?"

"No, thank you. I'm not in the mood right now."

"Why not?"

"Because I just took a shower and the sun's not out anymore and besides, that lake is filthy."

"Oh, c'mon."

"I said no, and please don't ask me again."

"Please. Pretty please."

"No. Why don't you go find someone your own age to play with?"

In the above example it wasn't difficult to keep track of who was speaking. One character spoke in short sentences, the other in longer sentences. And both characters had clear, opposing view points.

Having your characters use each other's names also helps your reader know who is speaking. If Joanne and Angie are having a conversation, and one character says, "Angie, will you pass the pickles?" your reader knows immediately Angie did not speak that sentence (unless you make it clear that Angie is talking to herself).

"Hey, Sarah, can I borrow your chain saw?"

"No, sorry."

"Why not?"

"Because I never lend out my tools, Michelle. You know that."

"But—"

"No buts. Sorry."

"Oh, c'mon, Sarah. You're not being fair."

"I'm sorry, Michelle. The answer is no."

Further suggestions: Pick up any novel or short story and notice how the author uses dialogue. Practice writing dialogues and vary the way you structure your sentences as much as possible. Try writing the following:

- a dialogue in which one person does all the talking
- a dialogue in which both people say the opposite of what they really mean

- a dialogue in which one person disagrees with everything the other person says
- a dialogue in which one person agrees with everything the other person says
- a dialogue in which two characters have extremely different speech patterns
- a dialogue in which one person tries to convince another person to do something
- a dialogue in which one person tries to convince someone to believe something
- a dialogue that takes place over the phone

Recommended reading: In "Penny For Your Thoughts," by Lenore Latta in *Word of Mouth, Volume Two,* edited by Irene Zahava, two people have a conversation in which their spoken words differ greatly from their thoughts. "A Perfect Day For Bananafish," by J.D. Salinger from his book *Nine Stories,* is a short story that begins with a phone conversation between a mother and daughter.

Conflict

Assignment:

Now we'll return to the characters we've been working with and practice writing dialogue with conflict. Conflict is the heart of dialogue. Conflict involves two characters who do not want the same thing.

There are many things to consider in writing dialogue with conflict. If this is a recurring conflict, when was the last time it was brought up? What are the characters' emotional states at the time of this dialogue? What went on in each character's day before the conflict arose? What has happened to the characters in the past that affects how they feel about this issue? How does the conflict escalate? And finally (and this is extremely important) what is the conflict behind the conflict?

Let's take an ordinary disagreement and explore the above questions. Jackie and Mira, who are roommates are arguing about whose turn it is to do the dishes. If Jackie and Mira had the same fight yesterday and the day before, this argument will probably be more heated than if the issue hasn't come up for months. If Jackie just got laid off from her job, her emotional state will be quite different from Mira's, who, let's say, just won the lottery.

Let's say, Jackie had to do the dishes every night after supper when she was growing up and her seven brothers never had to pick up a plate. It may be very important to Jackie that she be allowed to leave the dishes in the sink. It represents freedom to her. On the other hand, let's say Mira grew up in an alcoholic family where the dishes were never done. It may be very important to Mira to have the dishes washed right after supper every night, as it represents having some control over her life, which she never had as a child.

And most likely, Jackie and Mira aren't fighting about the dishes at all. Maybe Mira is fed up because she really wants to live alone but can't afford it. Maybe Jackie is frustrated because she's really in love with Mira but hasn't the guts to tell her. Who knows? You do. You the writer must know what your characters' hidden agendas are.

The last point I want to make about dialogue with conflict is that the conflict does not have to be resolved. Your characters do not have to live happily ever after. But something has to happen. If Mira and Jackie have fought about doing the dishes one hundred times, why are you writing about fight #101? What is revealed about the characters? What do they learn? How do they change? How don't they change?

Choose two characters who know each other and write a dialogue in which they have an ordinary conflict, such as doing the dishes. Keep in mind everything we have discussed about dialogue thus far. Don't worry too much about setting the scene; start right in with one character saying something to another.

Example: <u>Zelda and Deena fighting over doing the dishes</u>

"Grandma, sit down. I'll clean up." Deena pushed back her chair and started gathering up her dishes.

"You sit down and relax. There's only a few things to rinse out." Zelda didn't turn from the sink where she was wiping out the inside of a glass.

"Grandma, don't be silly. You should rest." Deena put her plate in the sink and tried to take the sponge from Zelda who held on fast. "C'mon, Grandma. You wouldn't let me cook, you can at least let me clean up."

"You'll clean up plenty when you're married and have a family. Now you should rest."

"Grandma, I don't know if Douglas and I are ever getting married. You think I'm not going to wash a dish until we decide?" Deena turned back to the table for the remaining plates and silverware. "You're so stubborn. Why don't you ever let anybody help you?"

Zelda shook the fork she was wiping off at Deena. "Is that a way to talk to your old grandma? Shame on you. I told your mother not to send you to that college there. You already finished one school, ain't that enough? Look how they teach you to talk to your own family. You should live at home until you're married yet, then you'll learn some manners. If you lived here, you could wash a dish. Now you're my guest."

Deena groaned. Why did her grandmother insist on living in the Dark Ages? No one stayed at home until they were married anymore. "Grandma, I'm twenty-three. That's old enough to be out on my own."

"You're a baby." Zelda poured some Joy onto her sponge and continued scrubbing. "I worry about you all the time."

"I worry about you."

"Me? You ain't gotta worry about me. I manage fine." Zelda put a cup in the dish drain.

"At least let me dry." Deena took a dish cloth off the back of a kitchen chair and reached for the cup.

"Don't touch nothing. I don't want you should break it."

"Oh, for God's sake, Grandma, I'm not a child." Deena flung down the dish towel.

"And I'm not a helpless old woman." Zelda's voice was as shrill as her granddaughter's. "I don't care if I'm eighty years old or one-hundred-and-eighty. I can still cook and clean up after myself."

Further suggestions: Practice writing dialogues that contain conflicts. Here are some suggestions:

- two people arguing about which movie to see or where to go out to dinner
- a couple fighting about where to go on vacation
- a teenager fighting with one of her parents about her allowance, her curfew, her clothes, etc.
- a couple fighting about having a child
- two friends arguing about what to get a third friend for her birthday
- two people arguing over directions
- a couple fighting about money
- a couple fighting about sex
- a couple fighting about spending time together
- two children fighting over a toy

Recommended reading: "Symbols," by Julie Blackwomon from her book *Voyages Out: 2*, is a short story that begins with two ex-lovers having a fight.

Secrets: Part I

Assignment

As we discussed in the section on monologues, all characters have secrets. Choose two characters who know each other, one of whom is keeping a secret from the other. Write a dialogue in which the second character tries to find out the first character's secret. Write the dialogue in such a way that the secret, though not revealed to the second character, is revealed to the reader.

Example:

Zelda opens the door and gives Deena a kiss on each cheek. "Hello, darling, how are you? I'm all ready to go, just let me get my coat."

"I don't know if I want to go." Deena follows her grandmother into the apartment, still feeling nauseous from the elevator ride. "Let me sit down a minute."

"What's the matter, you're tired?" Zelda stops with one arm inside her coat sleeve. "We don't have to go right away. I'll make us some tea."

"No thanks, Grandma," Deena calls out, but Zelda is already in the kitchen running water into the kettle. Tea will make me puke for sure, Deena thinks, sinking onto the couch. The only thing I could possibly handle right now are plain soda crackers but she'll know for sure if I ask her for that.

Zelda pokes her head out of the kitchen. "Why don't you put your feet up? This will only take a minute." She looks so pale, Zelda thinks as she gets out two tea bags. I hope she ain't catching a cold.

"Here, darling." Zelda brings two cups of tea into the living room. "What's the matter, are you sick?"

"I'll be fine." Deena turns her head, for even the smell of the tea is sickening.

"Do you have a headache?"

"No."

"A stomach ache?"

"No."

"A sore throat?"

"No."

"You're just tired?"

"Yes."

"What did you do last night?"

"Nothing." Deena sighs. If she only knew Douglas and I stayed up half the night discussing the abortion of her possible great-grandchild, she'd kill me.

"What's with all the one-word answers?" Zelda asks, staring at Deena. She's keeping something from me, Zelda thinks. "C'mon, darling, talk to your grandma. Whatever it is, it ain't so bad. Did you and Douglas have a fight?"

She always knows, Deena thinks, nodding her head.

"What did you fight about?"

Deena sighs, starts to speak and then changes her mind. "It was something really stupid, Grandma. We couldn't make up our minds about where to go eat."

Further suggestions: Write a second dialogue and have your characters switch roles. Now the second character has a secret she's trying to hide from the first character, who is trying to discover it. Again, reveal the secret to your reader, but not to the character who is trying to find the secret out.

Assignment

Choose two characters who know each other, one of whom has a secret. Again, write a dialogue in which the second character is trying to find out the first character's secret, but this time do not reveal the secret to the reader until it is revealed to the character. Notice how the tension builds differently when the reader knows the character's secret and when she doesn't.

Example:

"Listen, Deena, I got something to tell you." Zelda didn't kiss Deena hello on both cheeks like she usually did and Deena was instantly worried.

"What is it, Grandma, are you sick? What's wrong?" Deena, like everyone else in her family, always assumed the worst.

"No, I ain't sick. I'm fine. Come in, take off your coat already." Zelda closed the door behind her granddaughter and helped her off with her coat. "You want some coffee?"

"No, Grandma. Tell me what's on your mind."

"The news can wait. Come, I'll put on the water."

Deena followed her grandmother into the kitchen, a frown on her face. Was the expression "good news can wait"? Or was it "bad news can wait"? She wasn't sure.

"I got a fresh honey cake from the Avenue, oh, is that good." Zelda was making herself busy in the kitchen, setting out cups, forks and plates. "So, how are you, darling? What's new like this?"

"Nothing's new, Grandma. You're the one with news."

"My news is nothing, really."

"Then tell me."

"You're always in such a hurry, Deena." Zelda spooned some instant coffee into two cups. "Even when you was a baby, you couldn't wait for your mother to cross the room with the bottle. You'd start screaming the minute you saw it."

"Grandma." Deena sat down at the kitchen table and broke off a piece of honey cake with her fingers.

"It's good, no?" Zelda set the two cups of coffee on the table and sat down. "You want milk?"

"No. You know I always drink it black." She's definitely stalling, Deena thought. "So?"

"Ah, Deena." Zelda covered one of Deena's hands with her own. "What would you think if your old grandma took a little trip?"

"A trip? How long a trip?" Deena didn't know why, but her heart started to pound.

"Not so long a trip. Maybe a week."

"Where are you going?"

"Atlantic City."

"Atlantic City? Why would you want to go there?" Deena looked at Zelda closely. Something fishy was going on. "Who would you go with?"

"My neighbor, you know. Mr. Miller."

"Mr. Miller?" Deena's eyebrows shot up. "Why would you want to go anywhere with him?"

The smile Zelda had been trying to contain suddenly burst out all over her face. "We're getting married."

Further suggestions: Again, have your characters reverse roles so that now your second character has a secret she is trying to keep from your first character. Write a dialogue and reveal the secret to your reader at the same time it is being revealed to your character.

Practice writing dialogues that contain secrets and vary the ways in which the secrets are revealed to the characters and to the reader.

- a dialogue with a pleasant secret
- a dialogue with an unpleasant secret
- a dialogue with a tragic secret
- a dialogue with an insignificant secret
- a dialogue with a secret from the distant past

Recommended reading: In my own short story collection, *Secrets*, every story has a secret in it. In "Right Off The Bat," the secret is revealed to the reader and the person the character is addressing in the first sentence. In "What Happened To Sharon," Sharon's secret is revealed to the reader and the second main character at the same time, as the story goes on. And, in "One Night In The Middle Of My Lover's Arms," the narrator's secrets are revealed to the reader long before the second main character finds them out.

Time Out

Assignment

In this exercise, we will practice combining dialogue with monologue. Choose two characters who know each other and have a conflict. Write a dialogue between your characters, and then separate them so each character has a chance to have an internal monologue, exploring what they really think and feel. Then bring your characters back together to start another dialogue.

Example:

"Grandma, I'll go down to the Avenue. It'll take me five minutes to pick up some orange juice and milk." Deena already had her coat on and was looking for her keys.

"No, you don't go. I'll go." Zelda took off her apron. "Why should you go down and shlep? You rest. You work hard at school a whole year. Now you're on vacation. And besides, a carton of milk and a carton of juice is too heavy for you to carry."

"Grandma, please." Deena almost stamped her foot as if she were indeed the child Zelda was treating her like. "You stay here, it's cold out. I'll be right back."

"Put something on your head, you shouldn't get chilled with your hair wet like that." Zelda went into the closet to find a hat.

"I don't need a hat." Deena finally found her keys. "You want anything else while I'm going out?"

"No, I don't want you should carry so much. Here, take this." Zelda thrust a kerchief into Deena's hands. "And wait, take some money."

"I have money, Grandma. I'll be back in a minute."

"You sure I shouldn't come with you?" Zelda watched Deena put on her gloves.

"I'm sure." Deena opened the door and stepped out. "Be right back."

"Be careful how you cross the street."

"Grandma!" It was all Deena could do to keep from slamming the door. Honestly, she treats me like I'm still five years old, Deena thought as she punched the elevator button. What does she think I do at school, wait for someone every time I cross the street? Deena got into the elevator and jabbed "L" for lobby. She's so stubborn, she thought, walking through the foyer and out the building's front door. I wish she'd let me make breakfast once in a while. She works too hard. Deena looked up at her grandmother's window, where she knew she'd be standing, and gave a little wave.

Zelda waved back and watched Deena stop and chat with a neighbor before she crossed the street. So trusting she is, Zelda thought, turning from the window to set the table for breakfast. She'll get in trouble some day, the way she smiles at every stranger she meets. Not everyone is so nice, Zelda thought as she folded a napkin. There's crazy people everywhere and if anyone ever laid a hand on my Deena . . . Zelda busied herself with making toast to banish the thought from her mind. When the toast popped up, she put it in a deep dish and covered it with a silver lid to keep it warm. That's what I'd like to do with Deena, Zelda thought, turning back to the window. Cover her up so I could keep her warm and safe.

The front door opened and Deena flew in carrying a paper bag. "I'm back, Grandma. See, it only took me a minute. You didn't have to worry."

Zelda uncovered the toast. "Who said I was worrying? Come sit down and eat."

Further suggestions: Practice writing dialogues interrupted by internal monologues. Pay particular attention to what you discover about your characters as you read their thoughts. Also notice what your reader knows about your characters that they don't know about each other.

Recommended reading: In the short story, "Disasters," by Barbara Wilson from her book, *Miss Venezuela*, the two main characters, Laurel and Malcolm, open the story with a dialogue. Laurel then leaves the room and each character has an internal monologue, revealing to the reader how they really feel. And then the two characters reconnect and have another dialogue.

Trialogues

Assignment:

A trialogue is a conversation between three people. It is particularly important, when writing a trialogue, that you always make it clear to your reader who is speaking to whom. Having your characters use each other's names is one way to do this. Describing action helps as well (who is facing whom, etc.).

Choose three characters who know each other and write a trialogue involving them. Don't plan what they are going to say to each other; just let the conversation evolve naturally, as an actual conversation would.

Example:

Deena and Zelda were playing gin rummy when there was a knock at the door. "I'll get it," Deena said.

"You sit." Zelda was on her feet and halfway across the living room in two seconds flat. "Who is it?" she asked, pressing her ear against the door. Zelda no longer used her peephole, having read in the paper about a woman who had gotten shot through hers.

"It's Doris, from down the hall."

"Oh, Doris. Come in." Zelda stepped back to unlock the four locks on her door. "How are you?"

"I'm all right." Doris peeked into the living room. "You got company? I don't want to disturb you."

"Hi, Mrs. Reitman. Remember me?" Deena gave a little wave.

"Sure, I remember you. How are you, Deena?" Doris strode into the living room with Zelda behind her. "What are you playing, rummy?"

"Yeah, want to play?" Deena gathered all the cards together and began to shuffle them.

"Deena, I'm sure Doris has more important things to do than play cards." Zelda didn't ask Doris to sit down.

"Deal me in, Deena. I'll stay a little while." Doris settled down on the couch in Zelda's place. "So, what's new with you two?" Doris helped herself to a hard candy from the dish on the coffee table. "Any wedding bells in the air?"

"No. How many cards do I give out?" Deena started dealing, anxious to change the subject.

"Seven," Doris said. "Myra's granddaughter is getting married. You know, Myra from the fourth floor?" Doris looked at Zelda, who nodded. "And I hear she's three months pregnant."

"Go on," Zelda said, studying her cards.

"They're making a big wedding but they better hurry or she'll be showing." Doris picked up her cards and started arranging her hand.

"So, that's not such a big deal," Deena said, sorting through her cards. "Plenty of people get married when they're expecting a baby."

"What kind of nonsense are you talking?" Zelda sat down on the arm of the couch.

"It's not nonsense. I just don't see what the big deal is. You go first," Deena said to Doris.

"The big deal is a girl should get married first and pregnant second," Zelda said, keeping a close eye on Doris who was known to cheat.

"That's right," Doris said, discarding the three of clubs.

Deena's stomach was all in a knot. "What if I was pregnant, Grandma?" Deena asked, trying to sound casual.

"You?" Zelda turned her head to the side and pretended to spit three times. "God forbid. I wouldn't believe it. Don't even talk like that."

"Darling, don't make a joke like that. It ain't funny." Doris patted Deena's hand. "You'll make your grandma sick."

"It's not a joke." The words flew out of Deena's mouth before she could stop them. "It's true."

"What? What are you saying?" Zelda stared at Deena.

"I'm pregnant, Grandma."

"Oh boy." Doris couldn't hide her delight at hearing this new juicy tidbit of gossip.

"Oh, be quiet. You always bring trouble," Zelda snapped at Doris. Then she sighed and took her granddaughter's hand. "Deena, darling, what are we going to do?"

Further suggestions: Practice writing trialogues, and when that feels comfortable, try conversations between four people, five people, a dozen people. Try:

- a group of children at school
- a group of teenagers at a party
- parents and their child
- a group of co-workers at the office
- several people waiting for a bus
- three people involved in a love triangle

Recommended reading: The bulk of the short story, "Lunch With Harry," by Susan Minot from her book *Lust,* is a three way conversation between two women and a man having lunch together.

7

Point Of View: Whose?

Point of view refers to the style of narration you choose when writing a story. Quite simply, you must ask yourself who is telling the story. Is the story being told from the point of view of the main character? From a minor character's point of view? From the point of view of someone who is not a character in the story at all, but an outsider looking in?

Point of view can change a story in form or context. Depending on who is telling the story, certain details can be left out, others exaggerated. The emotional impact your story has on your reader is also affected by who is narrating your story.

For example, suppose a woman just had a fight with her daughter. Here is the mother recounting the story:

> All I did was ask Emily to put her clothes away when she got home from school. A simple, reasonable request. I asked her once, very politely, in a calm manner. I didn't want to start anything. When she ignored me, I asked her again, still keeping my voice low. When she did not respond to my second request, I picked up the pile of clothes (there must have been a week's worth) and quietly handed them to her without another word.

Now here is Emily's side of the story:

> The minute I walked in, my mother started nagging me to to put away my clothes in that screeching voice of hers. She asked me like ten times, before I even had a chance to take off my coat. I don't know what the big deal is; I would have gotten to it even-

tually. Besides it was just one pair of jeans and a sweater. Before I even got a chance to say, "Okay," she picked up my clothes and threw them at me. Then she turned around and gave me the cold shoulder for the rest of the day.

Same story, yet quite differently told from each character's point of view. Which version is correct? Both: each version represents that character's true emotional experience of that situation.

In the following exercises we will explore writing in different points of view: third person omniscient, first person, third person subjective, second person, and alternating points of view.

Third Person Omniscient:
The Know-It-All

Assignment

The third person omniscient narrator is not a character in the story: this narrator is the teller of a story she is not participating in. It is as if there is a person in the room with your characters at all times, telling the reader what is going on. Not only that, a third person omniscient narrator has super-human powers. She can read your characters' minds and has complete access to everyone's thoughts and feelings. She also has knowledge of everyone's dreams, memories and fantasies. She knows everything that has ever happened to any of your characters and can choose to reveal this information whenever it is appropriate to your story.

Write a scene between two characters you've been working with, using a third person omniscient narrator to tell the story.

Example:

After Doris left, Deena sighed quietly. This was one of the few times in her life she didn't look forward to being alone with her grandmother. She glanced at Zelda, who was still sitting on the couch. This is really bad, Deena thought. She didn't even get up to lock the door behind Doris.

Zelda didn't look at Deena, though she could feel her granddaughter's eyes staring at her. My Deena's not a baby anymore, Zelda thought, her body rocking slightly as she remembered holding her granddaughter for the very first time. Had it really been twenty-three years ago? Where had the time gone? Here she was all grown up, not even a virgin anymore. Zelda wanted to ask Deena if he had been good to her, was he gentle, did he say nice things, but she didn't. Instead she asked, "How do you feel?"

Deena blinked back her tears. "I'm all right, Grandma."

"You could move in here, darling. We could raise the baby together." Zelda's mind was already converting the living room into a nursery. The playpen could go here, the crib there . . ."

"Thanks Grandma, but I don't want to move back to Brooklyn." Deena was sorry to say it because she knew how Zelda felt about Brighton Beach. But Deena felt differently. As they said, it was a nice place to visit, but . . .

"Are you going to get married?" If Zelda couldn't help Deena take care of the baby, at least she could help her plan the wedding. She'd have to get married soon though, before she started to show.

"We're not getting married, Grandma." Deena didn't want to say the words, which stuck in her throat like a chicken bone, but she knew she had to even though they would break her grandmother's heart. "Douglas doesn't want to, and I'm not sure I want to either."

"Deena, when a woman has a baby, she should have a husband, too." Zelda spoke in a gentle voice, even though she felt like screaming.

"I'm not sure I'm going to have the baby," Deena said and then the room got so quiet both women could hear the pounding of their own hearts.

Further suggestions: Practice writing scenes with your characters, using a third person omniscient narrator to tell the story. Try not to favor one character over the other; give equal time to each character's thoughts, action and speech.

Recommended reading: "Tell Me A Riddle," by Tillie Olson from her book of the same name, is a magnificent story told by a third person omniscient narrator.

First Person: I'm Telling You

Assignment

In first person point of view, one of the characters in the story is also the narrator and tells the story. Whenever this character refers to herself, she uses the first person pronoun, "I." In fact, a story told in the first person is in essence, a monologue. A monologue that contains all the elements of a story: place, action, description, dialogue and so forth.

Since one character is telling a story that she is participating in, the story is told subjectively, from her point of view. The reader sees the story through this character's eyes and hears the story in this character's voice. In first person point of view, the narrator only has access to her own thoughts and feelings. She does not know (and cannot tell the reader) what is going on in any other character's mind unless that character chooses to tell her. If a character other than the narrator leaves the room, the narrator cannot tell the reader what that character is doing. The entire story is told from one character's point of view. Thus your reader will get to know that character very well.

Take the scene you wrote for the last writing exercise and rewrite it, using one of your characters as the narrator, who is telling the story in first person, using the pronoun, "I" when referring to herself.

Example:

After Doris left, I sighed quietly. I couldn't remember any other time in my life I was so unhappy about being alone with my grandmother. I looked over at her, sitting on the couch. This must be really bad, I thought. She didn't even get up to lock the door behind Doris. I continued watching her, but she wouldn't even look at me. I had no idea what she was thinking, but I knew she was trying to digest the news that not only was I, her baby, not a virgin anymore, but I was with child, as the saying goes. I was just about to say something, anything, when she spoke.

"How do you feel?" she asked.

I don't know why, but that made me want to cry. I had expected her to yell, scream, spit, throw things, but she didn't. I blinked back my tears. "I'm all right, Grandma."

"You could move in with me, darling. We could raise the baby together."

I looked around the small living room, trying to imagine it, even though I knew it would never happen. As the saying goes, Brighton Beach is a nice place to visit, but . . ."No thanks, Grandma," I said. "I don't want to move back to Brooklyn."

"Are you going to get married?"

I knew she would ask that. God, this is harder than I thought. "We're not getting married." I pushed the words out of my mouth even though they were sticking in my throat like a bone.

"Deena, when a woman has a baby, she should have a husband, too." I heard my grandmother's words, but they sounded fuzzy, like my ears were still clogged from an airplane ride. I took a deep breath and let the bomb drop.

"Grandma, I'm not sure I'm going to have the baby." I couldn't look at her after I said it and she didn't say a thing. The room got so quiet, all I could hear was the beating of my own heart.

Further suggestions: Rewrite the scene you just wrote, using your other character as the narrator, telling the story in first person, using the pronoun, "I" when referring to herself. Notice how the emotional impact of the story changes. Practice writing different scenes using a first person narrator.

Recommended reading: Rita Mae Brown's classic, *Rubyfruit Jungle,* is an example of a novel told in the first person.

Third Person Subjective:
The Alter Ego

Assignment

When using a third person subjective narrator, you are not as removed from your characters as you are with a third person omniscient narrator, yet you have more distance than when you are writing with a first person narrator, which is really like being inside one character's head. A third person subjective narrator acts like one character's alter ego. It is as if the narrator is standing right next to this one character at all times, recounting the story to the reader from this character's point of view. The narrator has access to this one character's thoughts and feelings; she also knows this particular character's history. Like the third person omniscient narrator, the third person subjective narrator is not a character in the story.

Rewrite your scene again, using a third person subjective narrator to tell the story from one character's point of view.

Example:

After Doris left, Zelda remained on the couch, not even bothering to get up and lock the door behind her. She didn't look at Deena, who sighed once, quietly, though she could feel Deena's eyes upon her. All Zelda could think about was the fact that her granddaughter was not a baby anymore. She remembered holding Deena in her arms for the very first time; how tiny she was, how soft her skin had been, like butter. How could that have been twenty-three years ago? Zelda couldn't believe it was possible, her Deena a woman, all grown up, not even a virgin anymore. Zelda's own wedding night flashed before her eyes and she wondered if Deena's had been so scary. And so wonderful. Was he good to you, darling? Zelda wanted to ask. Was he gentle? Did he say nice things? But Zelda didn't ask anything like that. Instead she said, "How do you feel?"

Deena blinked and Zelda could see the tears willed back, just as she herself so often forbade her own tears to fall. "I'm all right, Grandma."

"You could move in here, darling. We could raise the baby together." Zelda didn't know how they would manage, but they would manage. The living room could be the nursery. She looked around the room, already starting to plan. The playpen could go there, the crib there . . .

"Thanks, Grandma, but I don't want to move back to Brooklyn."

Sure, what would a young girl like Deena do in Brighton Beach, Zelda thought, no one here but old folks like me. It was probably just as well that she move in with Douglas. Though they should get married soon, before she started to show. That is, if they're gonna get married. I don't want to know, Zelda thought, but of course she asked. "Are you going to get married?"

"No, we're not getting married," Deena said, and Zelda winced inside. "Douglas doesn't want to, and I'm not sure I do either."

"Deena, when a woman has a baby, she should have a husband, too," Zelda said, keeping her voice gentle, though she felt like screaming.

"I'm not sure I'm going to have the baby," Deena said, and then the room got so quiet, Zelda could hear the beating of her ancient, broken heart.

Further suggestions: Rewrite this scene again, using a third person subjective narrator to tell the story from your other character's point of view. Practice writing scenes using this form of narration.

Recommended reading: My own book, *Good Enough To Eat*, is a novel that uses a third person subjective narrator to tell the story from the main character's point of view.

Second Person: You Know

Assignment

When writing from the second person point of view, the pronoun "you" takes the place of one of the characters in the story. This technique, when successful, is very powerful, for the reader feels like she is being directly spoken to. The reader feels like she is actually a character in the story, and all the events taking place are happening to her. The second person narrator only has access to the thoughts and feelings of the character being referred to as "you;" again this bonds the reader to that particular character.

Rewrite your scene, using a second person narrator, substituting the pronoun "you" for one of your characters.

Example:

You are sitting on the couch in your grandmother's living room, waiting for her to get up and lock the door behind her neighbor, who just left. Your grandmother does not get up. This is a bad sign, a very bad sign.

You wait for her to say something and wonder if you should speak first. For once, you, the original Chatty Cathy doll, can't think of a thing to say.

"How do you feel?" your grandmother asks. It is such a simple, caring question that tears spring to your eyes. You blink them back and answer, "I'm all right, Grandma."

"You could move in here. We could raise the baby together," your grandmother says. This is such a ridiculous suggestion, it almost makes you smile. You know it's ridiculous and you suspect your grandmother knows it, too. Still, you pretend to consider the offer before answering politely, "No thanks, Grandma. I don't want to move back to Brooklyn." That old saying flits through your mind: it's a nice place to visit, but . . .

"Are you going to get married?" There, she's asked the question you have been dreading and now you must answer it. You wish you were good at lying, but you're not. Especially to her.

"No, we're not getting married, Grandma," you say, though the words stick in your throat like the chicken bones from the soup your grandmother makes on Friday nights. "Douglas doesn't want to, and I'm not sure I do either."

Your grandmother speaks quietly, though you feel the tension behind her words. "Darling, when a woman has a baby, she should have a husband, too."

You make yourself say the words you know are going to kill her. "I'm not sure I'm going to have the baby," you whisper and then the room is so quiet all you hear is the sound of your own frantically beating heart.

Further suggestions: Rewrite your scene again, using a second person narrator, substituting the pronoun "you" for your other character. Practice writing scenes using a second person narrator to tell the story.

Recommended reading: "So You're Going To Have A New Body!" by Lynne Sharon Schwartz, from her book *The Melting Pot and Other Subversive Stories,* is an excellent example of the power a story can have when told from the second person point of view.

Alternating Point of View:
Taking Turns

Assignment

A story can be told from two (or more) points of view, alternating from character to character. This gives your reader a chance to hear each character's side of the story. You can tell a story using alternating points of view by using two (or more) third person subjective narrators, or by using two (or more) first person narrators. This technique is useful to get inside two (or more) characters' minds. It is also good for revealing information to the reader that the characters do not know about each other.

Rewrite your scene again, using alternating first person narrators to tell the story.

Example:

After Doris left, I waited for my grandmother to lock the door behind her. She didn't, so I knew she had taken the news hard. I sat and watched her, waiting for her to say something, anything.

I barely noticed Doris walking out the door. All I could think about was Deena, my baby Deena, lying in my arms so tiny, so soft, so warm. And now she tells me she's not a virgin anymore. I can't imagine it. I want to ask her what is was like, was he good to her, was he gentle, did he say nice things? Like my Murray, may he rest in peace, an angel he was, so scared I was. And not only that, she's pregnant already. Can it be, I'm old enough to be a great-grandmother? What can I say? "How do you feel?"

"I'm all right, Grandma."

All right, she tells me, how can she be all right? "You could move in here, darling," I say. "We could raise the baby together." I don't know how, but we'll manage. The crib can go over there by the television, the playpen can go there, we can get rid of the couch . . .

I am not going to cry in front of her. And I am not moving back home. I mean Brighton Beach is a nice place to visit, but I wouldn't want to live here. Besides, as they say, you can't go home again. "Thanks, Grandma, but I don't want to move back to Brooklyn." I watch her face crumble for a minute and then compose itself. "Are you going to get married?" she asks and I dread the answer I have to give her. I'm sure I'm one big, fat disappointment to her. "Grandma, we're not getting married," I say, though the words stick in my throat like chicken bones. "Douglas doesn't want to, and I'm not sure I want to, either."

I can't believe these words are coming out of the mouth of my own flesh and blood. Has she gone crazy? My Deena, always the good girl, every Chanukah she sends me a card, every Passover she comes home for the holiday, now a single mother she wants to be? I can't scream and carry on. I must be calm. "Deena," I explain gently, like she's two years old again, "when a woman has a baby, she should have a husband, too."

Oh God, she doesn't get it. I'm going to have to tell her. Why did I ever open my big mouth in the first place? "I'm not sure I'm going to have the baby," I say, and then the room is so quiet, I can hear the beating of my heart.

Further suggestions: Rewrite the scene again, using alternating third person subjective narrators to tell the story. Practice writing scenes using both types of alternating narrators.

Recommended reading: *Silver,* by Hilma Wolitzer, is a novel told in alternating first person points of view. The odd chapters are told in a woman's voice: even chapters are told by her husband. *This Place,* by Andrea Freud Lowewenstein, is a novel told from four points of view, using four third person subjective narrators. Each chapter is told from the point of view of either Telecea, a prisoner; Candy, also a prisoner; Ruth, a social worker; and Sonya, an art therapist.

8

The Elusive Plot

The plot of your story is the series of events that takes place. In other words, plot consists of what happens, what happens next, what happens after that, what happens after that, etc. Plot comes directly out of character. When you place specific characters in a specific situation, things begin to happen to them, events unfold, and your characters' destiny take shape. The plot of your story takes shape as well.

The Elusive Plot

The question I am asked most frequently about writing is, "How do you come up with your plot?" My answer always disappoints the asker of the question: "I don't." Plot is something that happens as your writing goes along. Plot emerges as your characters do things and as things happen to them.

Most of the time when I start writing, I don't have a specific story in mind. I usually start with an image or a character that interests me. I start writing about that image or character and see what happens. For example, my story "What Happened To Sharon" (from my book *Secrets*), begins with the main character dropping her contact lens into the kitty litter. I took this as a sign that this character was going to have a bad day. I didn't know all the terrible things that were going to happen to her that day; I just instinctively knew this incident was an omen and I continued writing to see what was to come.

Of course, I often have some idea of what I want or expect to happen in a story, but usually the story doesn't turn out that way, especially if I let the writing lead me, rather than try to control it. For example, I recently completed a novel called *In Every Laugh A Tear*, which tells what happens when a ninety-nine year old woman named Tzeydl is forced to move into a nursing home. My plan was that Tzeydl's granddaughter Shayna would convince Tzeydl to leave the nursing home and come live with her. After a few misadventures, Shayna would reluctantly return Tzeydl to the nursing home, both characters sadder and wiser than before.

So that was the plan and it all worked out fine except for one thing. When I got to the point in the novel where Shayna was supposed to convince Tzeydl to leave the nursing home, Tzeydl wouldn't go. She wouldn't budge, no matter how Shayna begged, pleaded, screamed and cried. And Shayna is not the type of character who would put sleeping pills in Tzeydl's coffee and abduct her against her will.

So there I was, at what I thought was the turning point of my novel, only my novel wouldn't turn. What could I do? Nothing, but keep writing and see what would happen to the characters next. And the writing moved me along to the climax and the conclusion of the novel, which I can now see worked out much better than the way I had originally planned it.

Plot is something that is obvious in hindsight. Here's another example. I recently wrote a short story called "Of Balloons and Bubbles," in which a character named Naomi, who is unsure whether she wants to have a baby or not, "borrows" Franny, a friend's two-year-old, to try out the idea of motherhood. I had no idea what Franny and Naomi's day was going to be like or what decision, if any, Naomi would make. What I did was put a particular character with a particular dilemma into a particular situation. Then I started writing to see what would happen.

Naomi's plan was to take Franny to get a Halloween pumpkin and then on to the park. Well, they got the pumpkin all right but on the way to the park they pass an Autumn Festival which Franny wants to stop at. I had no idea that Franny would be frightened by a clown, lose her balloon, almost get stung by a bee, demand to push her stroller by herself and almost ruin a whole table of stained glass decorations and have a complete temper tantrum on the way home. At the end of the story, Naomi returns Franny to her mother, and, after realizing, much to her amazement, that she's only been taking care of Franny for one hour, decides motherhood is not for her.

And so, now that I know the plot of the story and what it is building up to (Naomi's realization and decision), I take this knowledge back to the beginning of the story and rewrite the whole thing, bearing the plot and theme (meaning) in mind. I rewrite the story so that everything that happens to Naomi and Franny supports the emotional truth of the story. I make Franny have a two-year-old's day from hell. Everything goes wrong: she can't find the perfect pumpkin, she loses her balloon, her second balloon bursts, etc. And I exaggerate Naomi's character: she is completely baffled by the simplest tasks, such as how to retrieve Franny's bottle from the floor of the car while trying to keep the car on the road, and how to unfold a collapsible stroller. Everything that happens leads Naomi to the conclusion that motherhood is not all it's cracked up to be (but infinitely more).

My advice for figuring out plot can be summed up in one word: don't. Let go of controlling your writing: just write and see what happens. It's scarier, but it's also more exciting and it will result in better writing. Instead of planning a plot, put a specific character with a specific conflict into a specific situation and start writing. A plot will unfold. Trying to plan your plot is like trying to plan your life. Of course, you have some idea of what you want to happen, but more often than not it doesn't work out that way. Life hands you opportunities, disappointments and challenges you never dreamed of. Suppose I plan on spending a particular Saturday grocery shopping and then going to the movies. Fine. But what if I meet the love of my life in the produce aisle of Waldbaum's, squeezing grapefruits? What if I gather up all my courage and speak to this gorgeous stranger on the check-out line and what if we decide to go out to lunch?

Or, what if I back my car out of my parking space and ram right into a station wagon and spend the entire afternoon in the hospital? What if the person I injured turns out to be my boss's daughter and when I come to work Monday morning I get fired? In either case, I would never make it to the movies as I had planned. In either case, my life would change completely.

Writing is just like life. On any given day, you wake up with a plan in mind, but you really never know what's going to happen. Not every day holds such an extreme example as falling in love or being in a car crash (neither event is ever really planned). But an infinite amount of variables wait, to greet you every day: an unexpected phone call from someone you know or don't know; a chance meeting with a stranger; an impromptu lunch date with a friend; a change in the weather. Your life unfolds before you day by day, sometimes according to plan, sometimes not. Allow your characters that freedom as well.

Instead of trying to come up with an intricate and original plot, start writing about your characters and see what happens to them. There are no earth shattering plots when you come right down to it. Basically, most characters are born, go to school, go to work, fall in and out of love, grow old and die. That's it. Yet within this common plot, there is a vast, unlimited number of variations unique to each and every character. Focus on that, and the ordinary events in your characters' lives will unfold in extraordinary ways.

Remember Erich Segal's book *Love Story*, which later became a movie? We find out on the first page of the book, in the very first line, in fact, that the main character of the book is going to die. The plot is ruined, so to speak: we know the book's ending. Why read on? Because the what of the plot is not what concerns us; it is the how of the plot. How will this particular character live her life and how will she die? This is what intrigues us.

Concentrate on your characters when you write. Trust them and trust yourself. You will know when your story starts moving in the right direction. In the introduction to this book, I said that writing is 10 percent inspiration, 85 percent perspiration and 5 percent magic. The magic is something that cannot be taught, harnessed or controlled (that's why it's magic). You will know when the magic is present in your writing. It will pull you along on a journey of discovery and lead you places you never planned to go. After writing, I often look at a pile of pages and ask myself, "Where did that come from?" I truly feel like I didn't think of the story; rather it emerged on the page. The story came out of the writing; that is the magic at work. Trust it, and don't be too concerned with planning out a plot. Your plot will thicken, I assure you. When you finish a first draft of a story, reread it and write a summary of the plot that has emerged. Keep this plot in mind as you rewrite the story. Also, re-read some of your favorite stories (or try any that I have thus far recommended). After reading a story, write a summary of the plot. You may be surprised that some very interesting stories have very simple plots. Try writing a story with the same plot as one of your favorite stories. See how everything changes when you substitute your own characters.

9

What's the Story: Putting It All Together

The components of a short story have already been discussed: place, action, character, monologue, dialogue, point of view and plot. In this section we will tie everything together and wrap it up with a beginning and an ending, as well as offer a long list of ideas to keep you writing.

— *Beginnings, Middles and Endings* —

A short story has a beginning, a middle and an ending. All the components of the story we have already discussed comprise the middle of a story. Let us now turn our attention to beginnings and endings.

In journalism, the beginning of an article is called the "hook." In fiction as well, you want to "hook" your reader into your story at once. Your first sentence and opening paragraph are crucial, for quite frankly, if the first sentence is not interesting, why would anyone want to read the second? Your first paragraph is like a first impression, and you definitely want to impress your reader.

Whenever you start a story, you must bear in mind that most short stories don't start at the beginning; they start in the middle. A short story is like a visit to a character; the reader drops in at an important or interesting moment in a character's life. What would a story written about you right now start out with?

Example:

Lesléa sat on the maroon couch in her study, frantically scribbling in the loose-leaf notebook on her lap, while the clock ticked loudly, reminding her with every tock that her deadline was drawing near.

This story would not only find me in the middle of my day, it would also find me in the middle of a writing project.

A good beginning sparks your reader's curiosity. Taking the above example, the reader might wonder what is the character frantically scribbling about? How much longer does she have until her deadline? Will she make it? What happens if she doesn't?

Though your story starts with your characters in the middle of something, it is also the beginning of something: the start of your reader's relationship to your characters. Make them interesting and alive. Give your reader sensory images so your reader is right there with your characters.

Example:

"I scraped the runny fried egg off the bottom of the frying pan, slid it onto a piece of burnt toast, threw that onto a greasy plate and deposited the entire foul-smelling affair in front of my ex-lover, who was sitting at the kitchen table with that look on her face."

This opening sentence gives the reader several sensory images, plus piques her curiosity. Why is the narrator serving such a vile breakfast? Why is the narrator serving breakfast to this ex-lover? How long have the two characters been ex-lovers? How long were they lovers? What does "that look" imply? And most importantly, what is going to happen next?

Another way to start a story is with a piece of dialogue.

Example:

"I told you I was coming over today," Katherine said through the screen door. "Are you going to let me in?"

Immediately your character (and thus your reader) is right there in the middle of a situation. We want to know who Katherine is talking to, did she in fact tell this person she was coming over, is this other person happy to see her, has Katherine caught this person doing something she shouldn't be doing, and again, what is going to happen next?

An opening to a story should be just that: an opening. A door that your reader wants to step through.

Endings are just as important as beginnings. In fact, just as the start of a story isn't necessarily the beginning, the ending isn't the end either. It's the end of this particular moment in a character's life, but just as something ends, something else begins. Even if your character dies at the end of your story, her life ends, but at the same time, her death begins. When writing a story I don't plan its ending; usually the story draws to a close naturally. You will know when your characters are through with you. The story will come to a place that is surprising and predictable: surprising enough to make it interesting, and predictable enough to make it believable. Often the end of a story mirrors or echoes the beginning; the story has come full circle. In the chapter on plot, I mentioned the seventies' classic, *Love Story*. The book begins by informing the reader that the main character is going to die; the book ends with her death. In my own story, "Of Balloons and Bubbles," which I also discussed in the chapter on plot, the story begins with Naomi picking up Franny at her house, and the story ends with Naomi bringing Franny home: the story has circled back on itself.

As with beginnings, endings are vital to your story. Often your ending, or last impression, is what your reader will remember. It is not unlike a child learning the alphabet: the child recalls A-B-C and X-Y-Z but the middle tends to get murky. So you want to start strong and end strong. Again, an effective way to end a story is with a strong sensory image. You want to leave your reader with something she can walk away with, something she can see, hear, smell, feel or taste.

Example:

She turned and waved, her small hand fluttering like a lone leaf on a tree the last day of October, when everyone except me had the good sense to go home.

This image implies a feeling: loneliness. It is more effective to present the reader with an image that contains emotion, rather than to sum up the story.

Example:

She turned and waved to me and I felt lonely once again.

That ending falls flat: the narrator is telling the reader, rather than presenting an image that shows the reader how she feels.

The last sentence of your story can change its meaning completely. Some extreme examples are, "And then she died." "And then she woke up and realized it was all a dream."

Don't let your story fizzle out at the end. Write strong from your first sentence to your last. Present your reader with clear, strong sensory images that pull her into the story and stay with her long after the story has ended.

Look at your favorite short stories and novels and examine each one's first and last lines. See which first lines "hook" you immediately and notice which last lines leave a lasting impression.

— Assignments Galore: Keep Going —

Following is a catalog of assignments to inspire you to create stories. All of the suggestions are open-ended; start with the suggestion and see where it takes you. By now you know I am not the type of teacher (or writer) that works with formulas. I will not tell you to start your story with this, add this and this, end with that, and there you are. Instead, I will give you a place to jump off from; you take it from there.

As with all the other writing exercises, there is no wrong or right way to follow these suggestions. If you stay with the assignment for two sentences and then go off on a wild tangent, great. These are merely suggestions to get you going, as that seems to be most writers' biggest problem: where to start.

Here are eighty ideas to "jump-start" your pen, typewriter or computer:

1. Make a list of taboo subjects that you never write about for one reason or another (i.e., certain parts of your childhood, your sex life, your parents' sex life, etc.) Write a story about each item on your list.

2. Make a list of all the foreign words you know (i.e., hors d'oeuvres, sombrero, shalom). Write a story that includes all the words on your list.
   Recommended reading: My own story, "One *Shabbos* Evening" from my collection, *A Letter To Harvey Milk* was written after I made a list of all the Yiddish words I could think of.

3. Write a story set in another country about characters who do not come from that country. Make the setting alive and vital to the story.
   Recommended reading: Baby Driver, by Jan Kerouac, tells of a young American woman's adventures in Mexico. The first chapter's description of place is especially vivid.

4. Write a story in which you place a character you've been working with into a totally unfamiliar setting (though the setting is familiar to you). For example, I might place Zelda, the character I've

been working with, in the orange grove in Israel I described on page 47. See how your character responds to a new setting and situation.

5. Make a list of the following items:
     • an animal
     • a plant
     • a city or town
     • a piece of jewelry
     • a piece of clothing
     • a kitchen utensil
     • a carpenter's tool
     • a musical instrument
     • a tree
     • a bird
     • a vegetable
     • a color
     • a part of the body
     • a famous person

   Write a story that includes all these items.

6. Go to a Goodwill, Salvation Army, or used clothing store. Pick out an item of clothing that interests you and write a story about it.
   Recommended reading: "The Dress," by Jess Wells from her book *The Dress, The Sharda Stories,* tells of a woman's experience with a dress in a thrift store.

7. Write a story centered around an article of clothing that a particular character is very emotionally attached to.
   Recommended reading: "The Shawl," by Cynthia Ozick from her book by the same name, is an extremely powerful story of a child in a concentration camp and her attachment to a shawl.

8. Write a story that starts with a dream.
   Recommended reading: "Dictation," by Lisa Harris from *Word of Mouth: Volume Two,* edited by Irene Zahava, begins with one character having a dream that another character has dictated to her.

9. Write a story that begins with a character going to sleep.

10. Write a story that begins with a character waking up in a strange bed. *Recommended reading:* "Life On This Earth," by Ellen Gilchrist from her book *Light Can Be Both Wave and Particle*, begins with a man waking up on a stretcher.

11. Write a story that begins with two characters falling in love.

12. Write a story that begins with two characters falling out of love. *Recommended reading:* "Leaving Johanna," by Marian Thurm from her book *These Things Happen*, is a story about a man who no longer loves his lover of eight years.

13. Write a story that begins with a stranger coming to town. *Recommended reading:* "The Lesson," by Toni Cade Bambara from her book *Gorilla, My Love*, is a story about a new woman in town and the lesson she teaches a group of children.

14. Write a story about a character leaving on a trip. *Recommended reading:* "Mineola, Mineola," by Paula Martinac from *Voyages Out: One*, by Paula Martinac and Carla Tomaso, tells of a young woman leaving home for the first time.

15. Write a story that begins with a character getting a new job, or with a character getting fired. *Recommended reading:* "For Love Or Money," by Ruthann Robson from her book *Cecile*, is a story told by a woman who has recently been promoted.

16. Write a story that centers on a mother/daughter conflict. *Recommended reading:* "Home," by Jayne Anne Phillips from her book *Black Tickets*, concerns itself with a woman whose grown daughter has returned home for an extended visit.

17. Write a story that centers on a father/daughter conflict. *Recommended reading: Velocity*, by Kristan McCloy, is a novel that explores what happens to a young woman when her mother dies and the tension that emerges between her father and herself.

18. Write a story that begins with a character receiving a phone call. *Recommended reading: Loving Kindness*, by Anne Roiphe, begins with a woman receiving a disturbing phone call from her daughter.

19. Write a story that begins with a character losing something.
Recommended reading: Missing, by Michelle Herman, is a novel about an old woman who wakes up one morning unable to find some beads that are extremely precious to her.

20. Write a story that begins with someone finding something.
Recommended reading: "Other Lives," by Francine Prose, from her book *Women and Children First,* begins with a woman finding something unusual in her bathroom.

21. Write a story that begins with a character stealing something.
Recommended reading: "Lawns," by Mona Simpson, from the anthology *Deep Down,* edited by Laura Chester, begins with a character stealing letters.

22. Write a story that begins with a character receiving a gift.
Recommended reading: "No One's A Mystery," by Elizabeth Tallent from *The Available Press/PEN Short Story Collection,* begins with a young woman receiving a diary from her lover.

23. Write a story that begins with a character telling a lie.

24. Write a story based on a newspaper account. You have the "facts," now create a fiction with fully fleshed out characters and an emotional impact.
Recommended reading: "Looking For the Golden Gate," by Barbara Wilson from her book *Miss Venezuela,* is a story based on a newspaper account of a German man who gets off an airplane in Bangor, Maine, thinking he is in San Francisco.

25. Write a story that is based on a saying (i.e., "She who laughs last, laughs best.")
Recommended reading: "Forgiveness," by Rebecca Brown from the anthology *Passion Fruit,* edited by Jeanette Winterson, is the story of a character who not only says, "I'd give my right arm for you," but actually does.

26. Write a story that begins with a character receiving bad news (in person, over the phone, by letter, or by accident, such as reading something in the newspaper).
Recommended reading: "Kismet," by Jayne Loader, from her book *Wild America,* opens with a woman learning she is HIV–positive.

27. Write a story that begins with a character receiving good news.

28. Write a story that begins with a couple having a fight.
    Recommended reading: "The Dancing Party," by Mary Gordon from her book, *Temporary Shelter,* begins with a couple on their way to a party having a fight.

29. Write a story that begins with a couple making love.
    Recommended reading: "One Florida Night," by Cucu Lee from *Erotic Interludes,* edited by Lonnie Barbach, begins with a man and a woman making love.

30. Write a story in which the main character is a writer.
    Recommended reading: Zuckerman Unbound, by Phillip Roth, is my all time favorite novel about a writer.

31. Write a story narrated by a young child.
    Recommended reading: "Daddy," by Jan Clausen in her book, *Mother, Sister, Daughter, Lover,* is a story told by a little girl.

32. Write a story narrated by an old person.
    Recommended reading: "Be Not Forgetful of Strangers," by Natalie L.M. Petesch, from her book *Soul Clap Its Hands and Sing,* is a story told in the voice of an elderly woman.

33. Write a story in which one of the main characters is an animal.
    Recommended reading: "Henderson," by Meredith Rose, in *Through Other Eyes: Animal Stories by Women,* edited by Irene Zahava, is a story about a cow.

34. Write a story beginning with a character doing something she swore she'd never do.

35. Write a story that begins with one character trying to convince another character to do something.
    Recommended reading: "A Good Man Is Hard To Find," by Flannery O'Connor from her book by the same title, begins with a woman trying to convince her son to change his mind about a trip.

36. Write a story that begins with one character disobeying another.

37. Write a story that takes place in a moving vehicle.
    Recommended reading: "The Saints and Sinners Run," by Becky Birtha from her book *Lovers' Choice,* takes place on a bus.

38. Write a story that takes place in a bathroom.
    Recommended reading: "Forever Hold Your Piece," by Nancy Slonim Aronie, in *Word Of Mouth: Volume Two*, edited by Irene Zahava, is a short short story that takes place in a bathroom.

39. Write a story that takes place on another planet.

40. Write a story that centers around two characters eating a meal together.
    Recommended reading: "A Favorite Haunt," by Jess Wells from her book *Two Willow Chairs*, focuses on a couple celebrating their fifteenth anniversary at a fancy restaurant.

41. Write a story in which one of the characters is a celebrity.
    Recommended reading: Nona Casper's hilarious, "When I First Kissed Marsha from the Brady Bunch on the Lips and the Truth about Why the Series Ended," from *Voyages Out: Two*, by Julie Blackwomon and Nona Caspers.

42. Write a story in which a character unexpectantly meets someone from her past.
    Recommended reading: Then She Found Me, by Elinor Lipman, is a novel about what happens when a young woman who was adopted as a child is found by her birth mother.

43. Write a story in which a character unexpectantly meets someone from her future.

44. Write a story in which a character's wish unexpectantly comes true.
    Recommended reading: In, "His Family: A Fairy Tale Of The City," by M.J. Verlaine from his book *A Bad Man Is Easy To Find*, the main character's wish, after a little work, comes true in an unexpected way.

45. Write a story that takes place in ten minutes.
    Recommended reading: "Sister, Sister," by Maureen Brady, from the anthology *Word Of Mouth*, edited by Irene Zahava, is a powerful story that takes place in several minutes.

46. Write a short story that spans at least twenty years.
    Recommended reading: My own story, "The Gift," from my book *A Letter To Harvey Milk*, spans thirty years in a character's life.

47. Write a story that begins with a character remembering something.

48. Write a story that begins with a character forgetting something.

49. Write a story that begins with something breaking, shattering or exploding.

50. Write a story that begins with a character having an accident.
Recommended reading: "The Harvest," by Amy Hempel, from her book *At The Gates of the Animal Kingdom,* starts with a character almost being killed in a car crash.

51. Think of the happiest day of your life and write a story about it.

52. Think of the saddest day of your life and write a story about it.

53. Think of the scariest thing that ever happened to you and write a story about it.

54. Think of the most embarrassing thing that ever happened to you and write a story about it.

55. Think of something that made you absolutely furious and write a story about it.

56. Take a walk and come back and write a story.

57. Go for a drive and come back and write a story.

58. Write a story while listening to some music (try music with and without lyrics).

59. Write (or type) a story with your eyes closed.

60. Write a story with your right hand if you're a leftie or your left hand if you're a rightie.

61. Write a story in the form of a letter.
Recommended reading: "With Love, Lena," by Teya Schaffer, from the anthology *Women On Women,* edited by Joan Nestle and Naomi Holoch, is written in letter form.

62. Write a story in the form of a character's diary entries.
Recommended reading: "A Journal For The New Year Resolutions, Memos, Whimsies," by Natalie L.M. Petesch, from her

book *Soul Clap Its Hands And Sing*, is a short story in the form of a woman's journal.

63. Write a story that begins with a character giving advice.
    Recommended reading: "Girl," by Jamaica Kincaid, from her book *At The Bottom of The River*, is a monologue that gives advice.

64. Write a story that begins with a character seeing or hearing something she shouldn't.

65. Write a story that consists entirely of dialogue.
    Recommended reading: "The Knot," by Susan Minot, from her book *Lust and Other Stories*, is a series of short dialogues between a man and a woman.

66. Write a story with no dialogue in it whatsoever.
    Recommended reading: "The Woman Who Lives In The Elevator," by Claudia Kraehe, from *Word Of Mouth*, edited by Irene Zahava, is a story without any dialogue in it.

67. Write a story about a character having a fantasy. Experiment with blurring the lines between fantasy and reality.
    Recommended reading: "Where There's Smoke," by Tryna Hope from *Word of Mouth*, edited by Irene Zahava, is a story about a woman having a fantasy while waiting for a bus.

68. Write a story about two characters seeing each other for the last time.
    Recommended reading: "Some Blue Hills At Sundown," by Ellen Gilchrist, from her book *Light Can Be Both Wave and Particle*, is a story about a young girl seeing her boyfriend for the last time.

69. Write a story about two characters meeting for the first time.
    Recommended reading: "Romance," by Marian Thurm in her book *These Things Happen*, is a story about a man and a woman meeting at a mutual friend's wedding.

70. Write a story about a character falling in love for the first time.

71. Think of the sexiest experience you've ever had and write a story about it.

72. Think of the sexiest experience you would ever like to have and write a story about it

73. If you could see anyone in the world standing in your doorway right now, who would it be? Write a story about that person.
   Recommended reading: "Mother," by Grace Paley from her book *Later The Same Day,* is about a character who longs to see her mother standing in her doorway.

74. Write a story that includes directions or recipes in some way.
   Recommended reading: Sassafrass, Cypress and Indigo, by Ntozake Shange, is a novel that includes instructions and recipes, such as "To rid oneself of the scent of evil," and "Cypress' meal for Manhattan nights."

75. Write a story in which something that couldn't possibly happen, happens.
   Recommended reading: "The Baby Story," by Deborah Shea, in *Word Of Mouth,* edited by Irene Zahava, is an impossible story come true.

76. Write a story that begins with someone getting sick.
   Recommended reading: Spence and Lila, by Bobbie Ann Mason, is a novel that begins with a woman diagnosed with breast cancer.

78. Write a story that begins with someone getting well.

79. Write a story that begins with someone dying.
   Recommended reading: "The Thorn," by Mary Gordon, from the anthology *Fine Lines: The Best of Ms. Fiction,* edited by Ruth Sullivan, begins with the death of a little girl's father.

80. Write a story that begins with a character being born.
   Recommended reading: "X: A Fabulous Children's Story," by Lois Gould, in *The Woman Who Lost Her Names,* edited by Julia Wolf Mazow, is a story that starts with a child being born.

After Words:
The Pleasures of Publishing

I can't think of anything more exciting than seeing my name in print, whether that be on a book cover, in the table of contents of an anthology, or under a story of mine in a magazine. (I even get a little charge of seeing my name in the phone book!) If you share this yearning to see your name in print, read on for some helpful hints in getting it there.

The first thing to do is write, rewrite and rewrite once more. Don't send a piece of writing out until you are absolutely sure you have made it the best it can possibly be. Be proud of your work. You are offering an editor a piece of writing that you have spent time and energy on. I advise you to offer your work, rather than to submit it. To submit is to surrender to someone else's power or authority. To offer is to present something for consideration. A lot of writers feel powerless in the publishing world, where editors and publishers make decisions that can make or break a career. Yes, editors and publishers have a lot of power, but writers do, too. Editors and publishers have something we want—the ability to publish our work—but we have something they want, too: the work itself.

Let us consider the publishing of short stories. When sending a story out to a magazine, literary journal, or anthology, it is important to present your work as professionally as possible. Fiction must be typed and double-spaced. If you use a computer, make sure the print-out is very readable. Editors read hundreds, sometimes thousands of manuscripts every month. You want to present an editor with something that is easy on her eyes.

Enclose an SASE with your work. SASE stands for "self-addressed, stamped envelope." The envelope must have enough postage on it to ensure return of your work if it is not accepted. You may also send along a self-addressed, stamped postcard for the editor to use to acknowledge receipt of your work. Explain what this postcard is for in your cover letter.

Your cover letter should be brief and to the point (again, remember all editors get an unimaginable amount of mail every day). Some useful things to include in a cover letter are previous publications, literary awards you have won and literary organizations you belong to. If you are just starting to build up your publishing credentials, a letter like the one below will do:

Dear Editor:

Enclosed please find a short story entitled "Of Balloons and Bubbles," for you to consider for publication. I enclose an SASE and a postcard. Please use the postcard to acknowledge receipt of the manuscript, and to let me know when I can expect to hear from you.

Sincerely,

When can you expect to hear back from an editor? It varies. Usually, you can expect to get an acknowledgment postcard returned within a month. Unless stated otherwise, standard reply time for a story is three to four months. Be patient. Once you put something in the mail, let go of it and get back to your writing.

After about three months, if you haven't heard from an editor at all, contact her again. Write a brief letter stating that you sent a certain story to her three months ago and you are writing to inquire about the status of the story. Refer to your story by its title; unless you are extremely well known, an editor is more likely to remember the name of a story rather than the name of the person who wrote it. Again, enclose an SASE with this letter. (You can also send such a letter to an editor who told you via your acknowledgement postcard you would receive a reply by a certain date and that certain date is several weeks past.)

A question that frequently comes up in my writing workshops is the issue known as multiple submissions (which I rephrase as multiple offerings). Should you send the same story to more than one publication at a time? I advise against it. Editors are busy people. If an editor has read and considered your story, she has invested her time in it. If she accepts your story only to learn it has been accepted elsewhere, chances are she won't be very eager to read more of your work in the future.

My solution to the multiple offerings dilemma is to keep writing and thus have many stories to send out to a variety of magazines. At any given time, I have at least a dozen manuscripts in the mail.

Of course this means I have a lot to keep track of. Set up some kind of filing system for yourself so you know where each story is being considered at the moment, when you sent it out, and when an editor has told you to expect a reply. Also keep track of where each story has previously been sent. You don't want to make the mistake of sending a story somewhere where it has already been considered.

How do you decide where to send your work? Read, read, read. Become familiar with literary magazines and other publications where you are considering sending your work. Find magazines and journals where you think your writing will fit. I am not going to send a lesbian love story to *Field And Stream*, nor am I going to send an adventure story about fishing to *The Vegetarian Times*.

Familiarize yourself with possible markets for your work. Visit literary and feminist bookstores as well as the library, and study the magazines and journals you find there. Compile a list of publications you would like your work to appear in, write to each publication on your list and request their writers' guidelines (again, enclose an SASE). When you receive these guidelines, follow them. Some publications require the author's name on every page of the manuscript; others ask that the author's name not appear on the manuscript at all, but require a separate cover sheet. Some publications want stories twenty pages long or less, other publications put their maximum page limit at ten.

Another way to familiarize yourself with publishing possibilities is to read writers' magazines (see Writers' Resources in the Appendixes). These magazines have a section entitled Calls For Materials, where editors list what they are looking for. Perhaps an editor is putting together an anthology of stories written by women about First Dates and you've just written such a story. Or perhaps you like the idea of the anthology and decide to try and write a story for it.

Writers' magazines also list contests. Before entering a contest, send an SASE for each contest's writers' guidelines.

Another way to boost your writing career is to join writers' organizations (see Writers' Resources). Often these organizations send their members newsletters that contain interesting articles about writing as well as calls for materials and contest listings. Some writers' organizations hold conferences where you can meet other writers, as well as editors and publishers. Talk to these people. Networking can pay off in publishing just like in any other business.

Getting published is very exciting and gratifying. Having your work declined (I avoid the word rejected) is part of the process. Even after publishing a dozen books and over one-hundred stories and poems in anthologies and magazines, I still get my work returned to me in the mail. That's okay. It doesn't mean my work is bad or that an editor has used poor judgment. It means this was not a good match. This particular piece of writing did not meet this particular editor's needs at this particular time. When I get a story back in the mail, I send it right out to another publication. All writers deal with having their work accepted and not accepted on a regular basis. If you're going to be a writer, you'll have to get used to it.

Be patient and be persistent. If you work hard at making your writing the best it can be, present your work in a professional manner and keep sending it out, eventually you will see your name in print. Once you get published the first time, it does get easier (remember to mention your publication in subsequent cover letters).

Whether you get a story accepted the first time you send it out, or the one-hundredth time, it is a cause for celebration. Congratulate yourself, call your friends, have a party, toast yourself with champagne—and then get back to your writing.

Writers' Resources

Following is a list of resources for writers, including publications and organizations. I suggest writing to each publication, asking for a subscription form and a sample back issue, and writing to each organization to request information.

Publications For Writers

Associated Writing Programs Newsletter
Old Dominion University
Norfolk, VA 23529-0079

Feminist Bookstore News
P.O. Box 882554
San Francisco, CA 94188

Lambda Book Report: A Contemporary Review of Gay and Lesbian Literature
1625 Connecticut Ave. NW
Washington DC 20009

Poets and Writers Magazine
72 Spring Street
New York, NY 10012

Small Press Review
Box 100
Paradise, CA 95967

The Writer
120 Boylston Street
Boston, MA 02116

Writers' Digest
1507 Dana Avenue
Cincinnati, OH 45207

Organizations For Writers

Authors Guild and Authors League of America
234 W. 44th Street
New York, NY 10036

International Women's Writing Guild
Box 810 Gracie Station
New York, NY 10028

National Headquarters of Mystery Writers
236 W. 27th Street
New York, NY 10001

National Writers' Union
15 Astor Place 7th Floor
New York, NY 10003

Poets and Writers
72 Spring Street
New York, NY 10012

The Publishing Triangle
P.O. Box 114
Prince Street Station
New York, NY 10013

Society of Children's Book Writers and Illustrators
P.O. Box 296
Mar Vista Station
Los Angeles, CA 90066

Writing Conferences Especially For Women

Feminist Women's Writing Workshops, Inc.
P.O. Box 6583
Ithaca, NY 14851

Flight of the Mind: Summer Writing Workshops for Women
622 SE 28th Ave.
Portland, OR 97214

(Note: The International Women's Writing Guild holds writing conferences on a regular basis. Also, Poets and Writers publishes a listing of writers conferences.)

Selected Books on Writing

The following books focus on some aspect of writing: writing exercises, interviews with women writers, essays on writing and more.

Appelbaum, Judith and Evans, Nancy. *How To Get Happily Published*. New York: New American Library, 1978.

Bernays, Anne and Painter, Pamela. *What If?: Writing Exercises for Fiction Writers*. New York: HarperCollins, 1990 .

Bly, Carol. *The Passionate, Accurate Story: Making Your Heart's Truth Into Literature*. Minneapolis: Milkweed, 1990 .

Brande, Dorothea. *Becoming A Writer*. Los Angeles: Jeremy P. Tarcher, Inc., 1981.

Brandt, Kate. *Happy Endings: Lesbian Writers Talk About Their Lives and Work*. Tallahassee: Naiad Press, 1993.

Brown, Rita Mae. *Starting From Scratch: A Different Kind of Writers' Manual*. New York: Bantam, 1988.

Bryant, Dorothy. *Writing A Novel*. Berkeley: Ata Books, 1978.

Dillard, Annie. *The Writing Life*. New York: HarperPerennial, 1989.

Goldberg, Natalie. *Wild Mind*. New York: Bantam, 1990.

Goldberg, Natalie. *Writing Down The Bones*. Boston: Shambhala, 1986.

Hughes, Elaine Farris. *Writing From The Inner Self*. New York: HarperPerennial, 1991.

Killien, Christie and Bender, Sheila. *Writing In A Convertible With The Top Down: A Unique Guide For Writers*. New York: Warner Books, 1992.

Pearlman, Mickey and Henderson, Kathy Usher. *A Voice of One's Own: Conversations With America's Writing Women*. New York: Houghton Mifflin, 1990.

Plimpton, George. *Women Writers At Work: The Paris Review Interviews*. New York: Penguin, 1989.

Rico, Gabriele Lusser. *Writing The Natural Way*. Los Angeles: J.P. Tarcher, Inc., 1983.

Schnieder, Pat. *The Writer As An Artist: A New Approach To Writing Alone And With Others*. Los Angeles: RGA Lowell House, 1993.

Shelnutt, Eve. *The Writing Room: Keys To the Craft of Fiction and Poetry*. Atlanta: Longstreet Press, 1989.

Smith, Lucinda Irwin. *Women Who Write*. Englewood Cliffs, NJ: Julian Messner (division of Silver Burdett Press), 1989.

Snow, Kimberly. *Word Play, Word Power*. Berkeley: Conari Press, 1989.

Sternberg, Janet. *The Writer On Her Work*. New York; Norton, 1980.

Tate, Claudia. *Black Women Writers At Work*. New York: Continuum, 1989.

Ueland, Barbara. *If You Want To Write*. Saint Paul: Graywolf Press, 1987.

Welty, Eudora. *One Writer's Beginnings*. New York: Warner Books, 1983.

West, Celeste. *Words In Our Pockets*. Paradise, CA: Dustbooks, 1985.

Willis, Meredith Sue. *Personal Fiction Writing*. New York: Teachers and Writers Collaborative, 1984.

Women's Fiction Anthologies

If you want to write fiction, read fiction. Notice how other writers describe character, handle dialogue, etc. Often when you start to write, it becomes hard to read solely for pleasure. You begin to read as a writer, noticing what each author does with words. Reading anthologies is a good way to expose yourself to a wide variety of writing styles. If you come across a particular author you like, find out if she's published an entire volume of short stories, or a novel and read that as well. Here is a list of women's fiction anthologies to start with:

Agosin, Marjorie, ed. *Secret Weavers: Stories of the Fantastic by Women of Argentina.* New York: White Pine Press, 1992.

Allen Paula Gunn, ed. *Spider Woman's Granddaughter: Traditional Tales and Contemporary Writing by Native American Women.* New York: Fawcett Columbine, 1989.

Antler, Joyce, ed. *America and I: Short Stories By American Jewish Women Writers.* Boston: Beacon Press, 1990.

Barbach, Lonnie, ed. *Erotic Interludes: Tales Told By Women.* Garden City: Doubleday, 1986.

Bulkin, Elly, ed. *Lesbian Fiction.* Watertown, MA: Persephone Press, 1981.

Cahill, Susan, ed. *New Women and New Fiction: Short Stories Since The Sixties.* New York: New American Library, 1986.

Carter, Angela, ed. *Wayward Girls and Wicked Women: An Anthology of Subversive Stories.* New York: Penguin, 1986.

Carver, Ann and Chang Sung-Sheng, Yvonne, eds. *Bamboo Shoots After The Rain: Stories by Women Writers of Taiwan.* New York: Feminist Press, 1990.

Casey, Daniel J. and Casey, Linda M., eds. *Stories by Contemporary Irish Women.* Syracuse, NY: Syracuse University Press, 1990.

Conlon, Faith, da Silva, Rachel, and Wilson, Barbara, eds. *The Things That Divide Us: Stories By Women*. Seattle: Seal Press, 1985.

Corinne, Tee, ed. *Intricate Passions: A Collection of Erotic Short Fiction*. Austin, TX: Banned Books, 1989.

Erro, Peralta Nora and Silver-Nunez, Caridad, eds. *Beyond The Border: A New Age in Latin American Women's Fiction*. San Francisco: Cleis Press, 1991.

Esteves, Carmen C. and Paravisini-Gebert, Lizabeth, eds. *Green Cane Juicy Flotsam: Short Stories by Caribbean Women*. New Brunswick, NJ: Rutgers University Press, 1991.

Gibson, Mary Ellis, ed. *New Stories by Southern Women*. Columbia: University of South Carolina Press, 1989.

Gomez, Alma, Moraga, Cherrie and Romo-Carmona, Mariana, eds. *Cuentos: Stories by Latinas*. New York: Kitchen Table Press, 1983.

Goscilo, Helena, ed. *Balancing Acts: Contemporary Stories by Russian Women*. New York: Dell, 1989.

Hong, Zhu, ed. *The Serenity of Whiteness: Stories by and About Women in Contemporary China*. New York: Ballantine, 1991.

Kali for Women, ed. *Truth Tales: Contemporary Stories by Women Writers of India*. New York: Feminist Press, 1990.

Larson, Ann E. and Carr, Carole A., eds. *Crossing The Mainstream: New Fiction by Women Writers*. Seattle: Silver Leaf Press, 1987.

Martin, Wendy, ed. *We Are The Stories We Tell: The Best Short Stories by North American Women Since 1945*. New York: Pantheon, 1990.

Nestle, Joan and Holoch, Naomi, eds. *Women On Women: An Anthology of American Lesbian Short Fiction*. New York: Plume, 1990.

Niederman, Sharon, ed. *Shaking Eve's Tree: Short Stories of American Jewish Women*. Philadelphia: Jewish Publication Society, 1990.

Rafkin, Louise, ed. *Unholy Alliances: New Women's Fiction.* San Francisco: Cleis Press, 1988.

Sok-kyong, Kang, Chi-won, Kim and Chung-hui, O, eds.*Words of Farewell: Stories by Korean Women.* Seattle: Seal Press, 1989.

Sturgis, Suzanne, ed. *The Women Who Walk Through Fire: Fantasy and Science Fiction.* Freedom, CA: Crossing Press, 1990.

Sumrall, Amber Coverdale. *Lovers.* Freedom, CA: Crossing Press, 1992.

Tanaka, Yukiko, ed. *Unmapped Territories: New Women's Fiction From Japan.* Seattle: Women In Translation, 1991 .

Velez, Diana, ed. *Reclaiming Medusa: Stories by Contemporary Puerto Rican Women.* San Francisco: Spinsters/Aunt Lute, 1988.

Washington, Mary Helen, ed. *Black-eyed Susans Midnight Birds: Stories by and about Black Women.* New York: Doubleday, 1975 and 1980.

Zahava, Irene, ed. *Lesbian Love Stories* and *Lesbian Love Stories, Volume Two.* Freedom, CA: Crossing Press, 1989 and 1991.

Zahava, Irene, ed. *Love, Struggle and Change.* Freedom, CA: Crossing Press, 1988.

Zahava, Irene, ed. *My Father's Daughter.* Freedom, CA: Crossing Press, 1990.

Zahava, Irene, ed. *My Mother's Daughter.* Freedom, CA: Crossing Press, 1990.

Zahava, Irene, ed. *Word of Mouth: Short Short Stories,* and *Word of Mouth, Volume Two.* Freedom, CA: Crossing Press, 1990 and 1991.

Recommended Reading

Following is a list of all the short stories and novels and poems cited within the text of *Writing From The Heart:*

Aronie, Nancy Slonim. "Forever Hold Your Piece," in Irene Zahava, ed., *Word Of Mouth, Volume Two*. Freedom, CA: Crossing Press, 1991.

Bambara, Toni Cade. "The Lesson," in Toni Cade Bambara, author, *Gorilla, My Love*. New York: Vintage, 1981.

Beattie, Ann. "Janus," in Ann Beattie, author, *Where You'll Find Me*. New York: Macmillan, 1986.

Birtha, Becky. "Route 23: 10th and Bigler to Bethlehem Pike," and "The Saints and Sinners Run," in Becky Birtha, author, *Lovers' Choice*. Seattle: Seal Press, 1987.

Birtha, Becky. "Safekeeping," in Becky Birtha, author, *For Nights Like This One*. San Francisco: Frog In The Well Press, 1983.

Blackwomon, Julie. "Symbols," in Julie Blackwomon and Nona Caspers, authors, *Voyages Out: 2*. Seattle: Seal Press, 1990.

Block, Francesca Lia. *Weetzie Bat*. New York: Harper Collins, 1989.

Boucher, Sandy. "The Healer," in Irene Zahava, ed., *Hear The Silence: Stories by Women of Myth, Magic & Renewal*. Freedom, CA: Crossing Press, 1986.

Boucher, Sandy. "The Notebooks of Leni Clare," in Sandy Boucher, author, *The Notebooks of Leni Clare and Other Short Stories*. Trumansburg, NY: Crossing Press, 1982.

Brady, Maureen. "Sister, Sister," in Irene Zahava, ed., *Word of Mouth*. Freedom, CA: Crossing Press, 1990.

Brainard, Joe. *I Remember*. New York: Full Court Press, 1975.

Brown, Rebecca. "Forgiveness," in Jeanette Winterson, ed., *Passion Fruit*. London: Pandora, 1986.

Brown, Rita Mae. *Rubyfruit Jungle*. New York: Bantam, 1977.

Bryant, Dorothy. *Prisoners*. Berkeley: Ata Books, 1980.

Caspers, Nona. "When I First Kissed Marsha from the Brady Bunch on the Lips and the Truth about Why the Series Ended," in Julie Blackwomon and Nona Caspers, authors, *Voyages Out: 2*. Seattle: Seal Press, 1990.

Cisneros, Sandra. "Eleven," in Sandra Cisneros, author, *Woman Hollering Creek*. New York: Random House, 1991.

Clausen, Jan. "Daddy," in Jan Clausen, author, *Mother, Sister, Daughter, Lover*. Trumansburg, NY: Crossing Press, 1980.

Donegan, Patricia. "TELEPHONE I–XII," in Patricia Donegan, author, *Without Warning*. Berkeley: Parallax Press, 1990.

Frank, Anne. *The Diary of a Young Girl*. New York: Doubleday, 1952.

Gilchrist, Ellen. "Life on the Earth," and "Some Blue Hills at Sundown," in Ellen Gilchrist, author, *Light Can Be Both Wave and Particle*. Boston: Little, Brown and Co., 1989.

Gordon, Mary. "The Dancing Party," in Mary Gordon, author, *Temporary Shelter*. New York: Ballantine, 1988.

Gordon, Mary. "The Thorn," in Ruth Sullivan, ed., *Fine Lines: The Best of Ms. Fiction*. New York: Charles Scribner's Sons, 1981.

Gossett, Hattie. "womanmansion," in Hattie Gossett, author, *presenting . . . Sister No Blues*. Ithaca, NY: Firebrand Books, 1988.

Gould, Lois. "X: A Fabulous Children's Story," in Julia Wolf Mazow, ed., *The Woman Who Lost Her Names*. San Francisco: Harper and Row, 1980.

Harris, Lisa. "Dictation," in Irene Zahava, ed. *Word of Mouth, Volume Two*. Freedom, CA: Crossing Press, 1991.

Hempel, Amy. "The Harvest," in Amy Hempel, author, *At The Gates of the Animal Kingdom*. New York: Alfred A. Knopf, 1986.

Herman, Michelle. *Missing*. Columbus, OH: Ohio State University Press, 1990.

Hope, Tryna. "Where There's Smoke," in Irene Zahava, ed., *Word of Mouth*. Freedom, CA: Crossing Press, 1990.

James, Cherie. "Blood," in Irene Zahava, ed., *Word of Mouth, Volume Two*. Freedom, CA: Crossing Press, 1991.

Kerouac, Jack. *Visions of Cody*. New York: MacGraw-Hill, 1972.

Kerouac, Jan. *Baby Driver*. New York: St. Martin's Press, 1981.

Kincaid, Jamaica. "Girl," in Jamaica Kincaid, author, *At The Bottom Of The River*. New York: Vintage, 1985.

Kirshenbaum, Binnie. "Things To Do," in Binnie Kirshenbaum, author, *Married Life and Other True Adventures*. Freedom, CA: Crossing Press, 1990.

Konecky, Edith. *Allegra Maud Goldman*. Philadelphia: Jewish Publication Society, 1987.

Krahae, Claudia. "The Woman Who Lives in The Elevator," in Irene Zahava, ed., *Word of Mouth*. Freedom, CA: Crossing Press, 1990.

Kumin, Maxine. "In The Root Cellar," in Maxine Kumin, author, *House, Bridge, Fountain, Gate*. New York: Penguin, 1982.

Latta, Lenore. "Penny For Your Thoughts," in Irene Zahava, ed., *Word of Mouth, Volume Two*. Freedom, CA: Crossing Press, 1991.

Lee, Cucu. "One Florida Night," in Lonnie Barback, ed., *Erotic Interludes: Tales Told By Women*. Garden City: Doubleday, 1986.

Lipman, Elinor. *Then She Found Me*. New York: Washington Square Press, 1990.

Loader, Jayne. "Kismet," in Jayne Loader, author, *Wild America*. New York: Ivy Books, 1989.

Loewenstein, Andrea Freud. *This Place*. Boston: Pandora, 1985.

Martinac, Paula. "Mineola, Mineola," in Paula Martinac and Carla Tomaso, authors, *Voyages Out: 1*. Seattle: Seal Press, 1989.

Martz, Sandra, ed. *If I Had A Hammer.* Watsonville, CA: Papier-Mache Press, 1990.

Mason, Bobbie Ann. *Spence and Lila.* New York: Harper and Row, 1988.

Mayer, Bernadette. *Midwinter Day.* Berkeley: Turtle Island Foundation, 1982.

McCloy, Kristin. *Velocity.* New York: Washington Square Press, 1988.

Miller, Isabel. *Patience and Sarah.* New York: Fawcett Crest, 1969.

Minot, Susan. "Lunch With Harry," and "The Knot," in Susan Minot, author, *Lust.* Boston: Houghton Mifflin, 1989.

Moore, Lorrie. "How To Become A Writer," in Lorrie Moore, author, *Self-Help.* New York: Knopf, 1985.

Newman, Lesléa. *Good Enough To Eat.* Ithaca, NY: Firebrand Books, 1986.

Newman, Lesléa. *In Every Laugh A Tear.* Norwich, VT: New Victoria Publishers, 1992.

Newman, Lesléa. "A Letter To Harvey Milk," "Only A Phase," "One *Shabbos* Evening," and "The Gift," in Lesléa Newman, author, *A Letter To Harvey Milk.* Ithaca, NY: Firebrand Books, 1988.

Newman, Lesléa. "One Night in The Middle of My Lover's Arms," "Right Off The Bat," and "What Happened To Sharon," in Lesléa Newman, author, *Secrets.* Norwich, VT: New Victoria Publishers, 1990.

Notley, Alice. "Elephant and Ocean," in Alice Notley, author, *Waltzing Matilda.* New York: Kulchur Foundation, 1981.

O'Connor, Flannery. "A Good Man Is Hard To Find," in Flannery O'Connor, author, *A Good Man Is Hard To Find.* New York: Harcourt, Brace, Jovanovich, 1955.

Olson, Tillie. "Tell Me A Riddle," in Tillie Olson, author, *Tell Me A Riddle.* New York: Dell, 1956.

Ozick, Cynthia. "The Shawl," in Cynthia Ozick, author, *The Shawl*. New York: Knopf, 1980.

Paley, Grace. "Mother," in Grace Paley, author, *Later The Same Day*. New York: Penguin, 1985.

Paton, Alan. *Cry, The Beloved Country*. New York: Charles Scribner's Sons, 1948.

Petesch, Natalie, L.M. "A Journal For The New Year Resolutions, Memos and Whimsies," and "Be Not Forgetful of Strangers," in Natalie L.M. Petesch, author, *Soul Clap Its Hands And Sing*. Boston: South End Press, 1981.

Phillips, Jayne Anne. "Home," in Jayne Anne Phillips, author, *Black Tickets*. New York: Delacorte, 1975.

Piercy, Marge. "Six underrated pleasures," in Marge Piercy, author, *My Mother's Body*. New York: Knopf, 1985.

Prose, Francine. "Other Lives," in Francine Prose, author, *Women and Children First*. New York: Pantheon House, 1988.

Robson, Ruthann. "For Love Or Money," and "When The Sky Is Not Sky Blue," in Ruthann Robson, author, *Cecile*. Ithaca, NY: Firebrand Books, 1991.

Roiphe, Anne. *Loving Kindness*. New York: Warner Books, 1987.

Rose, Meredith. "Henderson," in Irene Zahava, ed., *Through Other Eyes: Animal Stories by Women*. Freedom, CA: Crossing Press, 1988.

Roth, Phillip. *Zuckerman Unbound*. New York: Fawcett Crest, 1981.

Rubin, Evan. "Preparing Dinner," in Judy Grahn, ed., *True To Life Adventure Stories, Volume Two*. Trumansburg, NY: Crossing Press, 1981.

Salinger, J.D. "A Perfect Day For Banana Fish," in J.D. Salinger, author, *Nine Stories*. New York: Bantam, 1964.

Sapphire. "i guess if i was a sound or if i was your woman," in *IKON, Second Series #3*. New York: IKON Press, 1984.

Sarton, May. *As We Are Now.* New York: Norton, 1973.

Sarton, May. *The Fur Person.* New York: Norton, 1978.

Schaeffer, Susan Fromberg. *Anya.* New York: Macmillan, 1974.

Schaffer, Teya. "With Love, Lena," in Naomi Holoch and Joan Nestle, eds., *Women On Women.* New York: Plume, 1990.

Schwartz, Delmore. "In Dreams Begin Responsibilities," in Irving Howe, ed., *Jewish American Stories.* New York: New American Library, 1972.

Schwartz, Lynne Sharon. *Leaving Brooklyn.* New York: Penguin, 1989.

Schwartz, Lynne Sharon. "Mrs. Saunders Writes Her Name To The World," in Lynne Sharon Schwartz, author, *Acquainted With The Night.* New York: Harper and Row, 1984.

Schwartz, Lynne Sharon. "So You're Going To Have A New Body" in Lynne Sharon Schwartz, author, *The Melting Pot and Other Subversive Stories.* New York: Penguin, 1987.

Schwartz, Patricia Roth. "Bodies," in Patricia Roth Schwartz, author, *The Names of the Moons of Mars.* Norwich, VT: New Victoria Publishers, 1989.

Schwerin, Doris. *Diary of a Pigeon Watcher.* New York: William Morris, 1976.

Shange, Ntozake. *sassafrass, indigo and cypress.* New York: St. Martin's Press, 1982.

Shea, Deborah. "The Baby Story," in Irene Zahava, ed., *Word of Mouth.* Freedom, CA: Crossing Press, 1990.

Simpson, Mona. "Lawns," in Laura Chester, ed., *Deep Down: The New Sensual Writing by Women.* Boston: Faber and Faber, 1988.

Solzhenitsyn, Alexander. *One Day in The Life of Ivan Denisovich.* New York: Dutton, 1963.

Stein, Gertrude. *Paris, France.* New York: Liveright, 1940.

Tallent, Elizabeth. "No One's A Mystery," in *Available Press/PEN Short Story Collection*. New York: Ballantine, 1985.

Terkel, Studs. *Working*. New York: Avon, 1972.

Thurm, Marian. "Leaving Johanna," and "Romance," in Marian Thurm, author, *These Things Happen*. New York: Washington Square Press, 1988.

Torchia, Joseph. *The Kryptonite Kid*. New York: Holt, Rinehart and Winston, 1979.

Tsui, Kitty. "Solitary Pleasure," in Irene Zahava, ed., *Finding Courage*. Freedom, CA: Crossing Press, 1989.

Tulloch, Lee. *Fabulous Nobodies: A Novel About A Girl in Love With Her Clothes*. New York: Harper and Row, 1989.

Verlaine, M.J. "His Family: A Fairy Tale Of The City," in M.J. Verlaine, author, *A Bad Man Is Easy To Find*. New York: St. Martin's Press, 1989.

Walker, Alice. *The Color Purple*. San Diego: Harcourt Brace Jovanovich, 1982.

Wells, Jess. "A Favorite Haunt," in Jess Wells, author, *Two Willow Chairs*. Chicago: Third Side Press, 1991.

Wells, Jess. "The Dress," in Jess Wells, author, *The Dress, The Sharda Stories*. Chicago: Third Side Press, 1991.

Wilson, Barbara. "Disasters," and "Looking For The Golden Gate," in Barbara Wilson, author, *Miss Venezuela*. Seattle: Seal Press, 1979.

Wolitzer, Hilma. *Silver*. New York: Ivy Books, 1988.

Yolen, Jane. *Briar Rose*. New York: TOR, 1992.

Zahava, Irene. "Alan Allen," in Irene Zahava, ed., *Word of Mouth, Volume Two*. Freedom, CA: Crossing Press, 1991.

About the Author

Lesléa Newman is a writer and editor with over twenty books to her credit, including novels, short story collections, poetry collections, non-fiction books, humor, and children's books. Her award-winning titles include *A Letter to Harvey Milk*, *In Every Laugh a Tear*, *Heather Has Two Mommies*, and *Out of the Closet and Nothing to Wear*. Ms. Newman's honors include a Massachusetts Artists Fellowship in Poetry, the *Highlights for Children* Fiction Writing Award, and the Parent's Choice Silver Award. Four of her books have been Lambda Literary Award Finalists. She has been teaching women's writing workshops since 1982 and frequently offers lectures and writing workshops at colleges, community centers and conferences across the country.

photo by Mary Vazquez